FUNDAMENTAL
SUSTAINABLE NETWORK
MARKETING TEAM

Beyond
the
Products

BeyondTheProducts.com

Ron Wilder

SimpleConnector.com

Beyond the Products
Fundamental Secrets to Build a Sustainable Network Marketing Team
By Ron Wilder
©2020 RW Intellectual Property, LLC
First Edition: October 2020

FINANCIAL DISCLOSURE STATEMENT
Please note that the information in this book is from the author's perspective and there is no guarantee you can make the amount of money discussed within this book because it depends on your individual efforts, abilities, and work ethic. That said, I know people who are making unbelievable amounts of money every month who initially had no idea this could happen for them when they started in their network marketing business.

Published by e-Tech Design Associates, LLC
Contact: www.SimpleConnector.com/contact
Book Cover Inspiration: Brier Mitchell
Book Layout Template ©2017 BookDesignTemplates.com
Ordering Information: Quantity sales. Special discounts are available on quantity purchases by corporations, associations, and others.
Contact: Ron Wilder, 4790 Caughlin Pkwy #777, Reno, NV 89519.
Beyond the Products/Ron Wilder —1st ed.
ISBN 978-1-7359178-0-1

Dedication

I dedicate this book to you, one of the hundreds of millions of home-based *solopreneurs* known as network marketers who are out of bed working before the kids wake up and then to bed late at night so you can achieve the dream of financial freedom.

You believe, before even your friends and family, that your purpose is much bigger than simply selling products and services to others. You are meant for greater things than your current life situation.

Persist on this journey with a strong personal "WHY" plus heart-centered action and you will manifest a great life, not only for you and your family, but for countless others you don't even know today.

And, when you have "arrived," your team leaders, who were once strangers in your life, will be your best friends on this planet because you will have touched their hearts and lives more than they could have ever imagined the day they met you.

TABLE OF CONTENTS

Foreword

The book that you are holding in your hands right now may be the secret sauce the network marketing industry has been missing since the beginning of MLM-time. Why do I say that?

I have been in the industry for over three decades and the CEO and Founder of The Network Marketing Magazine for the last 15 years. I have never come across a more comprehensive how-to guide to building a team for your business.

Ron Wilder has become one of my best friends in this confusing and noisy industry. As a top leader in a multibillion-dollar company he got to one of the highest levels, developing leaders deep down into his organization, by teaching team building. He not only taught about the great products, but as a business professional, Ron also taught *Beyond the Products!*

Ron has been a valued contributor to our magazine and is a frequent guest on our radio show. Ron has also been an invaluable contributor in the 27%er Success System. (www.27percenter.com)

If you are a 27%er who is serious about building a real, financially successful business, you and your team need to read and apply the principles within *Beyond the Products!*

George Madiou

CEO and Founder
The Network Marketing Magazine

> "If I would be given a chance to start all over again,
> I would choose NETWORK MARKETING."
>
> Bill Gates

Preface

This is the book I kept putting off. It was not high on my to-do list. But my business colleagues kept telling me I needed to write it because it could help so many people. Even though I knew this, I had so many projects on my plate that it kept getting delayed. Then, I read my own words about procrastination and realized it was time I practiced what I preached.

Many thanks to my friend and master motivator George Madiou, who pushed me to record an overview of my previous book for The Network Marketing Magazine and his 27 Percenter Success System (www.27Percenter.com). A short time ago, he wanted me to record a few chapters of my book for upcoming magazine issues.

That was the straw that broke the camel's back. I didn't want to record "old stuff" for him. I wanted to give him content I had yet to put down on paper because I knew it could help so many more people. Again, thank you, George, for encouraging me to write this book!

So, I cleared my desk, put on my headphones, plugged into my *"focus-at-will"* account... and started writing.

I am also forever grateful to Liz Wilder, my amazing bride of 16 years, who knows to leave me alone in my "cave" as I work into the wee hours of the morning. Going to bed at 3AM is not uncommon during this phase, but with no interruptions, so much gets done. Mahal Kita, habang buhay magpakailanman. (I love you forever.)

As I sit here writing (with headphones on in the middle of the night) I am grateful for all the life lessons and support my friends and business colleagues have bestowed on me.

A big thank you to my good friend, Bill *"one-more-thing"* Conrad, who has always encouraged me to write this book and has even threatened to write one, himself – Of course, he would have to stop squirreling to do that! 😊

Last, but not least, one person, who has helped me for years is Mary Jane Humes. She is my virtual assistant and has helped me in so many ways. She keeps me and my online training organized, reviews books and blog posts, and helps test my *Simple Connector* mobile app. She even edited this book for me! Mary Jane possesses an ever positive and caring attitude, and when I give her something to work on, I know it will get done. Thank you from the bottom of my heart for all that you do!

I am sure there are others whom I have forgotten to personally thank, and for that I apologize. Please know I am forever grateful you are in my life!

Keep smiling,

Oct 22, 2020 – 2:14 AM 😊

Introduction

The date was New Year's Eve, 2012, and the clock had just struck midnight. But I remember it like it was yesterday. We were $100,000 in credit card debt and hadn't made a house payment in over a year. Liz and I were sitting on our kitchen floor, hugging and crying. Was our life over? Were we going to lose it all?

Not exactly. About an hour earlier, we received a phone call with the message: "They have extended midnight so you can qualify." Were we after a home loan? Were we trying to escape to a deserted island? Nope. Because of the extension, we had just enough time to reach the rank of Diamond[1] in our network marketing company.

We couldn't believe it. We were elated! We had done it. And to be clear, when I say "we," I meant our entire team: both upline and downline. They were all involved, and we couldn't have done it without them. You see, you don't reach Diamond rank by yourself or by accident. It takes so much more than that. But I digress.

Were we financially free when we hit Diamond? Not yet, but we finally had the belief we could be if we just kept doing what

---

[1] Throughout this book, I use the term "Diamond" to refer to the top leaders of MLMs. Your MLM may have a different name for this rank. It is usually a leading MLM distributor who is earning 6-figures or more a year.

we were doing. A couple of weeks later, we received our first "five-figure" check in our MLM business and jumped with joy!

If you were to look back eighteen months from that date, you would have seen us in a quite different situation: we were in financial quicksand. Sure, we kept the appearances up like nothing was wrong, but the harder we struggled to get out, the deeper we sank. How did we go from broke and crazy-busy, trying almost everything to make money to Diamond? We worked both hard and smart and we followed the secrets and principles that I outline in this book.

Fast forward to today. We have no more debt, lots of free time and money to do what we want, when we want. This book, my apps, and my training course are examples of things I had time to create, because I now have the time do devote to such projects, thanks to the passive income from network marketing.

What is Your Situation?

Enough about us. Let's talk about you or someone you care about. Here are a few questions to see if I can help.

Please check all boxes that apply – REALLY!

- ☐ Are you stuck in your business?
- ☐ Does moving to the next rank seem almost impossible?
- ☐ Are you spinning plates all the time looking for orders at the end of the month?
- ☐ Do you have to do the work to build your "leaders'" legs rather than just your own to move to your next rank?

☐ Do you struggle to find a "WHY" that really motivates you to make changes in your life?

☐ Are you tired of holding all those little home parties with nobody showing up?

☐ Are you starting to wonder if YOU are ever going to make real money in your chosen MLM?

☐ Does your spouse put pressure on you to stop spending so much money on products?

☐ Do you struggle with distractions (chasing butterflies and squirrels)?

☐ Do you struggle with planning your week and sticking to your plan?

☐ Does looking at the compensation chart cause your head to spin?

☐ Do you want to find business builders rather than only customers?

☐ Do you struggle with following up with people you have prospected?

☐ Are you burning out trying to succeed?

☐ Are you overwhelmed with online tools or courses that promise network marketing success?

☐ Is COVID and the required social distancing slowing your belly-to-belly MLM prospecting success?

☐ Do you want to start building your business online?

If at least one or more answers are "yes," "YES," or "YEEESSS!!!," then this is the book for you because I discuss solutions to all them.

Your Past Does Not Matter

Maybe you have already tried to solve some of these challenges but have been unsuccessful. I am here to tell you not to worry.

If you want it badly enough, and you are willing to push past your challenges and limiting beliefs, you can have it. It took time for these challenges to happen in your life, and it will take time to get past them. However, they are ALL solvable! I wrote this book to help you acquire some alternate ways to put the problems in your rear-view mirror so you can finally get to the ranks (and lifestyle) you desire.

If you want a life you could only dream of, then TAKE ACTION to learn and practice the secrets that I have uncovered to build a successful network marketing business for yourself and the ones you love.

How to Read This Book

Owner vs. Reference Manuals

I see two types of nonfiction teaching books: owner manuals and reference manuals.

This book falls into the reference manual category. That means you can pick any chapter that interests you and dig in.

I know that distributors at every rank will be reading this book for tips of how to improve their business. If you feel you don't need help understanding the benefits of one topic, but want to know more about another, jump to that chapter. My feelings won't be hurt!

By the way, even if you feel YOU can skip a secret, consider reading anyway because one of your team members might need this information to either jump start their business or move it to the next level.

If you are looking for an "owner's manual" of how to build your network marketing business quickly, then consider one of my online courses. They start at week 0 with the pre-course basics and progress through to the end, teaching you step-by-step how to build quickly. Lessons are both on the web and in a mobile app so you can have it with you wherever you are as you go through the process.

Audio Version

I don't speed-read, and I love Audible because I can use my traveling university (my car) and become enlightened with new information, approaches, secrets, etc. while I'm sitting in traffic. That's how I learned Spanish in the early 1990s, sitting in Silicon Valley traffic listening and talking to Spanish tapes (yes, I got a few funny looks from other commuters). Amazingly, I can hold a simple conversation today from those tapes nearly thirty years ago.

A few months ago, I experienced something new. I had purchased a print book that came with a free audio version. I decided to listen to the book as I was reading it. WOW! Things stuck so much deeper. I was intrigued by the free recording idea because I don't usually buy a printed book and then pay again for the audio recording.

So, in the spirit of duplication, I decided to create a complete recording of this book that you can listen to with your Apple or Android phone. If you want, you can also try the approach that worked so well for me. Listen to it at 1.5x as you read if you prefer; you might be amazed by how fast you get through it.

If you download the audiobook chapters, you can listen to them when you are not on the internet (in an airplane, on a hike, or at a cabin in the woods). There is no longer any escape!

Note: The recording should be available sometime during November 2020.

QR Codes Throughout Book

Wherever you see a QR code (that funny square full of dots), you can use it to access additional information related to that chapter. If you are an iPhone user, pull out your camera and point it toward the QR code. A link will appear at the top of the screen. Click on that link to access the resource. Android users will need a QR code app. Sorry.

For those who prefer to use a desktop computer, I have added a direct link next to the code so you can type it directly into your desktop computer.

I Can Help You!

There are a couple of ways you can learn something new. Either through direct experience or from someone else.

Unfortunately for me, I tend to learn through direct experience, which is usually painful or at least the slowest way to learn something.

Congratulations! Since you are reading this, you are already ahead of the game. You will be able to skip a lot of the frustration of starting from scratch and not make the same mistakes I made when I started out.

Over the past twenty-five years I joined many network marketing companies, some you would probably recognize. In all except one of those businesses I spent more money on products than I made in income. None were successful at helping me become financially free until I figured out that it's NOT about how to sell more products. It is about helping people believe they can accomplish their dreams or make their problems disappear and then guiding them down the path to doing just that.

This is a much easier (and more profitable) way to build a network marketing business than trying to sell customers the next "amazing" product. As a result, I started to make more money than I spent—so much more that it led to our financial freedom. We now have more money than we need to live our lifestyle and I have the time to create things like this book, my courses, and apps.

In this book, I will give you some of the knowledge, skills, and tools (plus a dose of confidence) to convert your challenges into victories and happy times.

How My Biggest Fear Helped Me

When I started with the company that set us free, I was fearful of presenting in front of people. (I am an engineer, after all!) The thought of holding product parties felt too intimidating.

So, I read the company's compensation plan repeatedly until I understood how to get paid from this business adventure. I then figured out the most effective and efficient way to get paid the higher bonuses more quickly. It worked, so I taught it to my leaders and team so they could duplicate more effectively.

It was also clear that I had to attract others who wanted their own version of freedom if I was going to be successful. I wanted to create a passive income so I could do WHAT I wanted WHEN I wanted. In other words, I had to "duplicate" myself to make enough money so I could afford to free up my time. Little did I know my fear of presentations and minimal product knowledge would end up steering me towards the most effective way to make long-term stable income: focus on people, not products.

Choices, Choices, Choices

With all the books, audio recordings, videos, business training events, and courses already available, what can I possibly give you that you haven't heard before? Most MLM training revolves around the following approaches:

➢ **LIVE, SHARE, BUILD** - This type of prospecting has been around a long time and it is typically company-promoted because it pushes product sales. There are a lot of things to learn and the primary business growing activity is via home party/class product presentations. To me, the process feels like:

   ✓ **Live** = Buy the products and use them for yourself

   ✓ **Share** = Buy more products and share them with others, so THEY will use and then buy the products

   ✓ **Build** = Switch the mind-set of customers from buyers to sellers so they build their own team in the business, and thereby duplicate the Live, Share, Build process

➢ **HARDCORE PRODUCT SALES PROSPECTING** - This is a sell at any cost, product-centered approach that turns people off because the distributors typically push to convert the buyers into sellers. It feels "icky". The product(s) could be lotions or potions, financial services, vitamins, green cleaners, health juice, or a whole host of other products. When you see your relatives coming down your front walkway carrying a "product demo box" it makes you want to turn off your lights and pretend you're not at home. It is true that there are some cool products available from these companies, but quite often, we end up with cabinets and garages full of products, years after we have ended these "business opportunities."

➤ **HARDCORE BUSINESS OPPORTUNITY PROSPECTING -** This type of prospecting is like hardcore product sales except that distributors push the business opportunity above products. Quite often the products aren't even important and when you ask the name of the company, the distributor will side-step the question and start asking questions to distract you from your question. Why? Because the distributor knows that the company name will probably be associated with this type of sales approach. How many "business opportunity" meetings have you been invited to and attended in your life? Not fun, huh? 'Nuff said.

➤ **ONLINE FACEBOOK GROUP BUILDING** This type of prospecting requires an extensive pre-existing network of followers for quick results, it is hard to duplicate unless you have a lot of followers, it has a lower retention rate of customers, and requires lots of money and time investment for training and tools. Also, if you decide to advertise, it can get very expensive yet, produce few results. This approach is usually product centered.

➤ **PROFESSIONAL ONLINE WEBSITE** This form of business selling usually requires a lot of technical knowledge (or techy friends who really like you) to create websites, landing pages, opt-in forms, and auto-responders required for your "e-commerce funnel" prospects to opt in.

(Note: One exception is the use of online-MLM expert developed templates for websites, emails, and autoresponder campaigns to dramatically shorten your learning curve and expenses. – Check out *www.SimpleConnector.com/blog*)

The truth is that any of these approaches can work if your WHY is strong enough, you completely buy into them, and you closely duplicate what they teach. But you may have to sell your soul to the devil in the process. You've been warned!

So, How Can I Help You?

I suspect you are ready to learn how I can help YOU. After all, I'm sure you have heard plenty of "success stories" about other people but don't have a clue how to get the same results in your life. First, I'll explain how I discovered the secrets and then I'll list them out with a benefit of each.

A Contrarian Approach

I discovered early on (after intensely studying the compensation plan) that the REAL MLM money isn't from becoming a product salesperson; it comes from developing a <u>network of business builders</u> who develop their own network of builders, and so on. Duplicating network builders is a lot more profitable and creates a much more stable business in the long run than direct product sales.

This approach generally runs contrary to what the companies and top distributors usually teach new distributors. Again, they are looking for product flow volume to increase.

I have no idea why, but I tend to learn how things are done and want to optimize and automate things. The "network of builders" approach made more sense to me than a network of sellers if I wanted to quickly get to the higher bonus levels.

Along the way to Diamond, I learned things that helped me create a more stable long-term network marketing business and I shared these with my team. Now, I've decided to share them with you. It is time to prove that network marketing is a legitimate way to earn not only a little side income but freedom-creating levels of income.

My MLM Success Secrets

I have unearthed these secrets through the process of quickly building our business to Diamond and from guiding network marketers over the past few years through my web and mobile app-based training program.

Listening to and working with students on the weekly "planning your week" and "office hour" calls helped me understand why distributors were getting stuck in their businesses. My primary goal for the zoom calls was to suggest solutions and to validate their decision to build an MLM business as a foundation for their future lives.

It should go without saying that there a lot of common givens about how to build a network marketing business. Things like "duplicate your leaders" and "the fortune is in the follow up" are not secrets. So, I have not included them in my secrets list.

The list below includes the name of each secret and a benefit to learning it. I've included a chapter for each in this book.

➢ Build a people-centered biz for a stable long-term income

➢ Lead, rather than manage your team to stop spinning plates

➢ Build fast for faster $$$, team motivation, and momentum

➢ Prioritize your time to achieve your results and goals

➢ Find the "WHY" that will push you to build your business

➢ Get "uncomfortable" to accelerate your business growth

➢ Transform your fears into confidence – Yes, CONFIDENCE!

➢ Use "icky-free", honest prospecting methods to feel ethical

➢ Follow-up can be easy by using online automation tech

➢ Understand how you get paid to maximize your profits

➢ Pick a good MLM company for long-term passive income

➢ Avoid 13 time sucks to build your business faster

➢ Relax and stay happy so you can enjoy your journey

Understand and implement these secrets to build your business, create an amazing team of leaders, and enjoy the fruits of your labor.

CHAPTER 2

An Overview of the Secrets

There is a saying: "If you want to learn what successful people know, hang around with them, and do the things they do. The odds of your own success will then be higher." So, what's stopping you? There are a lot of successful people in network marketing. Isn't it time you learned what they know about success and start doing it? Trust me; if you do what they do, you'll be hanging with them too, on the beaches of the world. Ready to learn some secrets?

Times and Business Training Have Changed

Depending on how long you have been "doing" network marketing, you may have been exposed to one or more ways to build your business that have worked for different Diamonds and above but may not have worked for you.

To be clear, I'm not saying their techniques don't work. They do; otherwise, they would not have reached Diamond. The challenge I hear from many is that there is just too much information available. With the abundance of videos and courses out there, most don't know where to start. They're overwhelmed.

My Secrets

Below is a summary of the twelve secrets I've discovered to build a successful network marketing business. Each is covered in a separate chapter.

Secret #1: Build a People-Centered Business

Diamond and above distributors prospect for their personal enrollments differently than most new distributors. Sure, they still share the products, but they quickly move to more business-builder types of questions because they are looking for new leaders for their team. Most distributors are focused on the products and therefore ask different types of questions.

Why don't Diamonds teach new people how to do what *they* do? I think it is because both types of prospecting require different knowledge and skills and most Diamonds find it easier to teach what they learned in the beginning. My experience is that looking for business builders right from the beginning can be easier to duplicate than to convert buyers into business builders.

Secret #2: Lead, Don't Manage

Successful Diamond and above leaders don't "manage" their teams. They lead them by inspiring their team to want to follow in their footsteps. They focus on finding builders who want their own version of freedom.

Secret #3: Build Fast

Reaching the initial leader bonuses of $2000/month is not easy. But, there are many benefits for not only reaching this level but doing it quickly. You will make more money faster if you grow fast. In fact, some of your company bonuses might even disappear if you are too slow!

Unfortunately, many distributors take months and even years to reach the $2K/month level, which makes it much tougher to reach higher rank levels because team momentum is not there unless all of your leaders growing at the same rate.

Secret #4: Prioritize Your Time

Time flies when you're having fun. But it also flies when you are lost in the distractions of daily life. Time is our most valuable resource, yet we waste it every single day. Some of the topics include how five minutes can be enough time for many business tasks; how to plan your week based on results, rather than activities; the multitasking myth; and learning how to manage distractions.

Secret #5: Your SMART WHY™ is Your Fuel

It is sad to say that most people haven't found a WHY that motivates them to get the results they want. I'll explore why this is the case, and I'll help you understand the difference between WHYs and DREAMs. Finally, I'll give you a step-by-step process to figure out your own SMART WHY™ strong enough to motivate you to bounce out of bed in the morning to get stuff done.

Secret #6: Comfort Stops Progress

People are creatures of comfort.

- ➢ We love that comfortable recliner.
- ➢ We enjoy spending time doing things we like to do.

> ➤ We spend our money on things before can afford them.

> ➤ We stay in relationships that aren't healthy.

Why? Because it is too uncomfortable to change. Yet, if we don't change, then — wait for it — NOTHING WILL CHANGE! Surprise, surprise! If you want to change, then you will need to get uncomfortable. In fact, you will learn to get comfortable being uncomfortable. Strange concept, I know.

This secret is about how to get uncomfortable and push past your limiting beliefs to become the better version of yourself you so richly deserve. Don't wait until you're sixty or seventy to start this! The sooner you start, the better your life will be!

Secret #7: Transform Fear to Confidence

It is sad how much fear blocks us from achieving the greatness we deserve. Fortunately, almost all our fear is in our mind. After all, we don't have saber-toothed tigers waking us from our sleep in our caves anymore.

Unfortunately, that old reptilian brain is still deep inside our mind, and it pops its ugly head out at the worst times. I discuss some of the common fears that plague distributors and discuss how to solve them to create more confidence while building your business.

Confidence is very attractive, and as you increase it, you will draw more of the people into your business who will want to work with you, helping you create the business you only hoped you could have. I also discuss common prospecting objections and how to handle them.

Secret #8: Practice "Icky-Free" Prospecting

If you have ever felt "icky" while prospecting to build your business, check out this secret. I show you how to transform your prospecting approach so you can build with more confidence.

Also, learn how to tell your story with a simple set of steps, and help prospects craft a believable plan to transform their current lives to ones they deserve--on your team!

Secret #9: Follow-Up Can Be Easy

I was going to call this secret "The Fortune Is in the Follow-Up." However, this isn't a secret. So, I dug deeper to find a real secret: How to make follow-up easy. Most of the distributors and salespeople I know, hate the follow-up process. That's because they are not using a secret weapon: technology that automatically follows up with their prospects in an effortless way.

I'll touch on manual follow-up techniques and then dig into how to leverage the computer inside your smart phone to capture leads, automatically send them information they want, and even invite them to reconnect, as you stand next to them.

Secret #10: Understand HOW You Can Get Paid

As much as you want to share the products (i.e. give out samples), you're in a business, not a charity. So, it makes sense that you should know how you will get paid if you want to maximize your profits. Yes?

Understanding different types of compensation plans various MLM companies offer and the various phases of MLM business growth will give you clarity of how far you want to aim in your business.

Secret #11: Pick Your MLM Company Carefully

Although understanding how to get paid is important, other things about your chosen company are more important if you want long-term passive income. If there are any missing pieces, then you or your company won't be successful in the long-term. Use my checklist to see if you're on the right track.

Secret #12: What NOT to Do to Build Fast

I have seen many new and even seasoned distributors waste incredible amounts of time on ineffective activities they think will help them grow their business. That is the reason one of my favorite topics is what NOT to do to build fast! I want to warn distributors to recognize and avoid these activities before they engage in them or to re-evaluate if they are doing them now.

As you've probably gathered, because I'm a contrarian, I like to debate assumptions of success that are taught by most leaders. Some of the "NOT TOs" might surprise you at first glance (e.g. "don't buy business cards"). After you read my reasons, though, you will begin to see why it is essential to avoid these activities if you want to build your business quickly. There are thirteen of them. Hmmm. That was a pure coincidence. Or was it? Enjoy!

Bonuses

Building Your MLM Business During COVID

The global pandemic has changed the way most business builders prospect since social distancing kind of gets in the way of belly-to-belly prospecting. It's time to rethink online approaches to build your network marketing business.

This bonus chapter provides some guidance of how to augment your traditional MLM prospecting with an online component. Using duplicable templates of online MLM experts and simple, low-cost tools, you could on the internet in a few hours instead of months.

How to Stay Happy and Enjoy the Journey

There are plenty of super achievers who are never satisfied. They win second place but are depressed because they didn't come in first place. Distributors can fall into the same trap, lamenting that they didn't make their targeted rank before the annual convention even though they joined only a few months earlier.

This chapter will put things into perspective so you can be happy and enjoy your journey to whatever rank you are after.

This video lesson is from week 7 of one of my courses, and I included it because so many students received value from it. Keeping a positive mindset is a vital part of growing a strong and successful business.

Free Audio Version of this Book

As I noted earlier, everyone who buys my book also gets a free audio version. This should help make the information even more accessible to you. The recording should be available during November 2020.

Free Trial of *SimpleConnector*™ CRM Mobile App

One of the most powerful ways to follow up with prospects and stay in touch with new friends and team members is by using automation to help you. I've also included a free trial of *Simple-Connector*™: a patent-pending mobile app you can use both for belly-to-belly prospecting and internet-based lead capture and follow-up.

CHAPTER 3

Secret #1:
Build a People-Centered Business

I f you had a choice of people to add to your team, which type would you prefer?

Distributors who buy and sell products and teach others to do the same

OR

Distributors who prospect people who want to up-level their lives and buy their own products from their business

If you find yourself even slightly undecided, keep reading to better understand the difference and how to shift your perspective if you want to build a sustainable network marketing business.

I define the first category of people as being product-centered: they focus on the buying and selling of products. I define the second category of people as people-centered. Also, before you scream that this is an MLM pyramid scheme, please realize that I prospect using a hybrid of the two approaches, and all bonus money originates through product flow. So, you can start breathing again!

The main differences of my method are:

✓ How I leverage the products to make the initial connection and

✓ How I bring up the business conversation

My goal is to shift the focus to the prospects and their life goals by leveraging the products to start the conversation.

People vs. Product-Centered Prospecting

Let's get into the language of product-centered vs. people-centered prospecting so you can better understand them and how they are fundamentally different at a core level.

Product-Centered Prospecting

Product-centered distributors include practices like:

☐ Sharing the products

☐ Holding group product demonstration classes

☐ Doing home parties to introduce the products

☐ Pushing corporate BOGOs (*Buy One, Get One free*)

☐ Offering your own end-of-month BOGOs and specials

☐ Focusing on monthly product sales rather than rank

☐ Focusing on selling products, rather then focusing on adding distributors

☐ Holding make-and-take classes

☐ Doing farmers' markets, street fairs, and health fairs

☐ Selling your personalized adaptations of products

☐ Using tech tools to determine prospect's product needs

☐ Spending time memorizing product uses

☐ Building product selling websites

☐ Recommending products for ailments (eeek! — FDA)

☐ Becoming the product expert in your community

☐ Big, empty frontlines in your organization

☐ "Icky" feeling when trying to convert buyers into builders

☐ Small monthly bonus checks ($10's to $100's)

Can you see the pattern? Everything revolves around buying and selling products. These activities would seem like logical ones to do as a product-based company distributor, and we have been taught and encouraged to do just that if we want to grow our business.

However, my experience has shown it is much more effective to look for business network builders rather than customers.

People-Centered Prospecting

Let's contrast this with people-centered prospecting, which includes practices like:

☐ One-on-one meetings rather than group meetings (great if you have a fear of being in front of people, like I did)

☐ Going out and making friends

☐ Learning social styles to better relate to people

☐ Dream building

☐ Talking about possibilities

☐ Planning clear paths for people to improve their future

☐ Helping people develop confidence

☐ Asking more personal financial questions to give more effective answers

☐ Building lifestyle websites

☐ Discussing how to make money with the comp plan

☐ Creating a network of builders

☐ Receiving bigger monthly bonus checks

As you may have noticed, people-centered prospecting focuses on finding people who are looking for a better future for themselves rather than on finding people wishing to buy and sell products for health, wellness, or other reasons. We use the language and an approach that is more (you guessed it) people-centered. The secret is how we blend this business-building language with our product business.

The goal of people-centered prospecting is to get to a personal one-on-one conversation with the prospect to find out if they might be someone you'd like to work with.

It could start by talking about the products, but would quickly shift to a business focus or start right with the business conversation with a simple question like "Would you like this year to be a better year than last year?" Hopefully, this could trigger an interesting conversation. Honed questions can shift the conversation from products to people and help you find the team builders you are looking for.

From the first meeting, this approach could leverage the products to start a people-centered conversation to find prospects who are open to developing an extra side income or full-time income to change their future. What could that look like for them? But, the sooner you can get onto the topic of the business rather than the products, the sooner you will find those elusive business builders.

Don't worry if you think this would be uncomfortable. We have plenty of pages left in this book to help you become more confident in the process. Check out Secret #8 ("Practice 'Icky-Free' Prospecting") for more examples of how to connect with your prospects.

Trust me; when you find them, you will think you have found kindred spirits to run with on your journey to Diamond and beyond.

Realize that all serious business-building distributors will always buy products. They will be very consistent and won't have to be prodded at the end of the month to place an order. They will understand that if they want to get paid, they must put in their minimum order if required to qualify for their bonus payments. Moreover, as they experience more and more products, they will eventually have and use them all, even if they don't join with the largest starter kit. Product knowledge naturally happens over time. Once your builders experience more and more of your company's products, they will organically want more for themselves so the minimum monthly orders will become part of their lives. The truth is that the more products they experience, the harder it will be to *limit* their orders to the minimum because they are so liked!

How Successful Leaders Prospect

If you ask most successful Diamonds and above how THEY prospect people for their personal enrollments, they will tell you they do one-on-ones rather than home product demo classes. Why? Because they can more effectively connect with prospects who want to build the business and less on those who want to buy and sell products. This approach to prospecting allows them to tap into the higher bonuses all MLM companies pay out."

Unfortunately, most leaders teach us how to do product classes from day one, explaining that it's the way to go if you want to build your business. All you have to do is convince your friends (like herding kittens) to come to your house (which has to be cleaned up) and then teach them about products (shaking in your boots the first few times or more). The goal of the class is to sell them a kit, but honestly, any sale will do if you can enroll them as a customer.

Over time, though, many of the people who come to those classes don't continue to buy, let alone become your business leaders. Why? Because they saw how uncomfortable you were and didn't want any part of it. Sure, some do stick, but it's an uphill battle.

Promoting the Business Opportunity

I have always promoted the business opportunity along with the products on a one-on-one basis. I do use the products as the conversation starter, but I always focus on how a home-based business could provide them with the possibility to make their lives better on the financial front.

Why one-on-ones? Because I can have more in-depth conversations with them to find their WHY. I also let them know I would love to help them break free of whatever is holding them back and to guide them toward the greatness they deserve. Maybe it is as simple as helping them find a way to buy a new car or pay for daycare or quit their job in six months to a year. I help them craft a step-by-step map, showing them how to get there. I also let them know I believe in them, because that faith can give them the confidence, they need to make it happen. I assure them that I'm there to help them stay on track as their personal business coach. (I also mentor in the beginning if they have not made a firm commitment.)

So, why are leaders teaching distributors both from the stage and in their courses to hold product classes in their homes to enroll people if that's not how they do it themselves? I came up with four reasons:

➢ It is what they learned when they first signed up
➢ It is what most leaders say to do
➢ It is easier to teach people how to sell products rather than to teach them how to prospect for business builders
➢ Diamonds don't want to go against other leaders
➢ It is what the MLM company recommends

Just to set the record straight, these approaches do work, and there are plenty of Diamonds to prove it, but in my opinion, it is just a slower path to get to the higher levels, and when you get to the higher levels, you don't use it anymore.

One-on-ones are much more effective. If you personally know any Diamonds or above, ask them to tell you honestly how they prospect for their personal enrollments. Then ask them why they don't teach what they do! (And hand them a copy of this book. ☺)

Isn't This a Ponzi Scheme?

Okay, I must get this out there before I get all of the companies and high-level distributors mad at me. If you think I am not saying to buy products, that is not the case.

For at least a couple of reasons, every serious business builder will buy products without being prompted:

- ✓ Builders need products for their own health, wellness, or other reasons.
- ✓ Builders know there is usually a minimum monthly purchase requirement to receive a bonus, so all serious builders do their monthly orders (Note: Not all MLMs require personal purchases to earn bonuses.)

I'll bet that if you are a business builder and I offered you $150 cash not to order this month, you'd reject the offer. Why? Because you KNOW the value of placing the order. True?

How much time could you save at the end of the month not having to hunt for people to put in their minimum orders so you can get your bonus? I know Diamonds who struggle with this because they are focusing on product-centered building. Developing a network of builders, rather than customers, solves this problem because their builders will always put in their orders to qualify for *their* bonuses.

So, you can breathe again. We are not building an illegal Ponzi scheme by signing up people with the promise of making money from everyone you sign up and no product flow. Every business builder will buy products, so they get paid.

Are You Open to Change?

After reading this chapter, will you continue to talk only about the products when you prospect? I know they're cool and amazing and powerful and life-changing, but are you open to learning how to prospect for different types of people using a different approach? Would you be open to having a bunch of business builders on your team who are focused on helping to empower others to become business builders? How would this change your current lifestyle or enable you to manifest your transformation to the new, improved version of yourself?

Take a few moments and write down your thoughts.

_____

_____

_____

_____

_____

_____

_____

_____

_____

_____

CHAPTER 4

Secret #2:
Lead, Don't Manage

A re you frustrated that your business "leaders" are not building, let alone leading?

Do you find yourself spinning plates at the end of the month, trying to get people to place orders needed for you to qualify for matrix or rank bonuses?

Do you struggle to get your leaders to engage in the business?

The way you build your business is what causes all these challenges. You are probably *managing* your team, rather than *leading* them.

Your Team Is an All-Volunteer Army

Before I explain how to lead your team, let's dig into some ways you may be managing them: (Check all that apply to the way you build your business.)

☐ Calling team members to remind them to put orders in on the last day of the month

- ☐ Telling them to have weekly mentoring or coaching calls with you
- ☐ Reminding them to come to your business training class or Zoom training calls
- ☐ Pushing them to go to conventions and other events
- ☐ Holding them accountable to things even if they didn't ask to held accountable
- ☐ Telling them how they should build and structure their business
- ☐ Placing orders within their leg to create structural or rank bonuses
- ☐ Enrolling and placing people on their teams and then guilting them to build since they are making money because of it

Can you think of any other examples from your own business? Examples would include things you:

- ☐ Tell them to do
- ☐ Push them to do
- ☐ Do it yourself "for" them

Most of the time, your motive for taking these steps is to move their business along the path <u>you</u> want it to move.

Below, list some of the things you do. (No one else needs to see this list, so be honest!)

I tell my leaders:

_____

_____

_____

I push my leaders to:

_____

_____

_____

I do the following myself to qualify my leaders for their bonuses:

_____

_____

_____

If you haven't already seen the pattern, all the above things are all about you and your success and your desires. It is NOT about how your leaders will benefit.

The last list was sort of a trick question. Sure, they might get bonus, but many times, your REAL motive is to get <u>your</u> personal bonus.

Why isn't managing your team effective? Because your team is an all-volunteer army. You are not paying them a salary to work for you and do what you want. <u>The reality is that you work for them</u>, especially when you are getting them started! Your goal should be to empower them to be self-sufficient business builders so that you won't have to bug them every month to "do their part" to earn their bonuses. You will receive your time back many times over in the long run.

Your team is an all-volunteer army. Lead them, don't manage them!

The leaders in my business only call when they have a question or are trying to solve a problem. I don't have to call them weekly or monthly to push them to do things. They see the value in solving most of the issues on their own. That's how I have so much time these days to create things like this book, my courses, my apps, and other projects.

Make It About Them

The acronym WIIFM stands for "What's In It For Me?" It comes from the perspective of others when you are talking, texting, emailing, or messaging them. If they don't see the value for themselves in most of the communications, they will probably stop picking up the phone or answering the texts, emails, and messages. Have you ever been ghosted by one or more of your team members? If they are still alive, they probably realized that the messages didn't benefit them, and after a while, they decided to spend time with others who did provide value or friendship for them. It is not that they don't like you, but they're busy people, just like you. Have you ever noticed when YOU have ghosted someone else? Maybe you stopped picking up the phone, answering texts or messages, or contributing to their Facebook wall. If you are honest with yourself, you'll realize it is because you didn't see the value in doing so.

We are all busy people and our free time is valuable, so we become gatekeepers to other people trying to access our time. If you want to shift things so that people start communicating with you and maybe even start building again, then you get to begin leading them, not managing them, since the goal of leading is for you to GIVE them value, not receive it.

So, how do you lead them? By inspiring them to want to do it themselves.

Leadership is about providing value to them and not the other way around. They will be more interested in connecting with you if they feel you care about them, and in turn, they will care about you.

Head vs. Heart

Did you notice I used words *like, feel,* and *care* above? These are words of the heart, rather than the head. Words like *think, right, fair,* and *accountable* are "head" words, which can get in the way of developing relationships.

Remember that MLMs are relationship-businesses. Both parts are required, and if you forget the relationship component, your business will suffer.

Letting your team know you care about them could include things like these:

- ➢ Girls' or guys' night out with NO talk about the business
- ➢ Send them a personalized card IN THE MAIL letting them know how much you value having them in your life
- ➢ Leaving a voicemail, text, message, or email just thanking them for being your friend
- ➢ Sending them thoughtful random gift in the mail
- ➢ Posting something nice about them in your Facebook group (recognition goes a long ways)
- ➢ Sending or giving them a birthday card or small gift

➤ Taking them out for lunch when they accomplish something that was important to them

Many distributors tend to focus almost exclusively on the business side of things, especially those who are on a fast track to one rank or another. Can you think of some nice relationship-building activities you could do to inspire your team? Add a few.

_____

_____

_____

_____

_____

_____

_____

Now, add some of these to your calendar to remind you to follow through with it. If you need help, you could use our *SimpleConnector* mobile app to schedule reminders to complete these activities.

If you inspire your team members by letting them know how much you care for them, value them, and are available to help them out, they will want to associate with you, and they will follow you to the ends of the earth supporting your dreams too.

CHAPTER 5

Secret #3:
Build Fast

When you decided to build your business, did you want it to grow fast or slow? I ask this because most people tend to develop slowly. I decided I wanted to build quickly, so I studied the compensation plan to see how I could maximize both my own and my team's profits. Since network structure bonuses generate most of the money, I realized that is where I needed to focus my energy and not on product selling. (I will review compensation plans in Secret # 10: "Understand How You Can Get Paid.")

In this chapter, I will list out some of the benefits of building fast. However, even though it makes sense to build fast, many people don't do that, so I'll also explain why it takes some people longer than others.

$2000/month is Simple, But Not Easy

In essence, reaching $2000/month is simple: Just look at your compensation plan and add people who buy products until you reach the required volume in your chosen month and make sure you place your own minimum order, if required.

That's it! Boom!

So, it is simple, but is it easy? It seems easier for some people than others, but a lot of that comes from various factors, including:

- The number of people in your network of friends or people who follow you
- Your comfort level meeting new people
- Previous network marketing experience
- How bad you want it

The most significant factor, in my opinion, is how bad you want it. If your WHY is giant, then you will work harder to make it happen. Moreover, WHYs come in all shapes and sizes. The trick is finding the WHY that will motivate YOU. There is a lot of information about finding your WHY out there, but much of it doesn't go deep enough or is too broad. Secret #5 shows into how I help distributors dig out a meaningful and motivating WHY.

Benefits of Building Fast

When you achieve a beginning leadership level of $2000/month, you will experience many benefits. Some of the benefits are tangible, and others are intangible. All of them are worth having and will help to motivate you to keep pushing onward.

So, what are some of these benefits?

The obvious one is the tangible benefit: you will start making thousands of monthly dollars in bonuses rather than tens or hundreds of dollars. For some people, this is motivation enough, but there are many intangible benefits:

> Personal feeling of accomplishment. You've "joined the club" and share a bond with other distributors who have previously reached that level, knowing you all pushed through the challenges and made it happen.

> You might qualify and be recognized as a leader in your company with lots of cheering, photos, and team-building comradery. (It's FUN to be a leader!)

> The confidence you can repeat it and show your team leaders how to do what you did.

> Belief in your ability to make real money in your chosen MLM company, knowing you will be able to drop-kick your job to the curb someday and build the life you want for you and your family.

> Proof for your significant other that this isn't just a money-sucking "little MLM business"; this one feels delicious — yes?

> Sometimes you will have access to special leader account managers in your company who can help you with your business-building challenges — a very nice benefit, indeed!

> Special access to annual events like conventions (with other distributors at your level) so you can dash to the front and grab better seats.

> ➤ An invitation to your company or team's leadership event, where you will learn techniques that leaders like you can use to build a more effective team.
> ➤ A foundation of builders to help you reach higher ranks like Diamond and above.
> ➤ A VERY proud team of people (many of whom have been with you from the start) who look to you for inspiration and gain the confidence they can do it too.

So, you see, building fast and becoming a leader is a BIG DEAL!

Also, it doesn't happen by accident. It takes a commitment to the process and requires you to put in the time and other resources to make it happen.

But Wait, There's More!

Building your business to a $2000/month level quickly has additional monetary benefits you will not achieve by building slowly. When you build fast, you create momentum in your business and reach higher ranks faster. Everyone is excited that you reached your level, and they want it too. Helping your team members rank up so they can leave their jobs is really fun and rewarding!

Another interesting data point is that that it doesn't matter if you build to $2000/month fast or slow. The *stick rate* is the same! What does this mean? Once you reach that level, your chance of staying there or reaching higher ranks is the same. So, go fast to enjoy the other benefits mentioned earlier.

One final reason to build fast is that your WHY happens faster. The faster you build, the quicker you can achieve the results you are after. Your WHY becomes much more believable. You can see it happening so much sooner!

Knowing all this, why would you ever build slow?

Why Most Distributors Take So Long

Some distributors see $2000/month as an elusive level. They suffer from a lack of confidence. They don't believe they can achieve it. We reached $2000/month in just over a month, which helped build our foundation for Diamond that happened the following year, which helped us get out of debt faster. The result was we had more time to start doing what we wanted to do because we had a significant regular monthly income. We could afford to go on the company incentive trips. We could also eat out more, and we stopped worrying about every dollar we spent, knowing that those dollars weren't adding to credit card debt.

Going Diamond also allowed me to use some of my time to develop my online courses which have helped lots of distributors on their journeys, as well as the apps to allow them to build when they are out and about.

Like us, some distributors climb to $2000/month very quickly and enjoy the benefits. Others take a long time or never even make it, even with all the significant advantages. Here are some of the reasons I see that hold them back:

☐ **No strong, motivating WHY** - Your WHY is your fuel. Without it, progress slows dramatically! That's why the next chapter explores how you can create a strong, motivating WHY.

- ☐ **Bad coaching from sponsors** - Let's face it, if a motivated Diamond enrolls you, you will probably have better one-on-one coaching than if you were enrolled by a brand-new distributor friend of yours who was enrolled by a friend of hers a week ago. There are a couple of solutions here if you want to build fast. First, reach upward to your closest Diamond leader and ask for one-on-one time with that person to help you build quickly. Second, consider enrolling in an online course to help you get clear on what you need to know to succeed. Some courses, like mine, include support groups and calls you can tap into to help keep you motivated and give you cool success tips along the way.

- ☐ **Overwhelm** - Some leaders are teaching too much, too quickly. Beware if your sponsor simply recommends going to the company website to watch some videos. New distributors need to know which videos to view and when to view them. Otherwise, they may become overwhelmed.

- ☐ **Unrealistic expectations** - Let's face it, sometimes distributors want you on their team so badly they might stretch how easily you can build your network marketing business and make money. Some of them will even be so focused on signing up new people, they might not be able to provide the support you'll need to build fast. As a result, it is up to you to figure out whom to get help from to make it happen. Sometimes it gets frustrating when it is taking a long time. Don't give up! If your enrolling sponsor is not able to meet you where you are at, ask if they would be willing to connect you to their upline. If they are not open to that, then it is up to you to connect with an upline leader to get proper guidance. Joining a training program, as mentioned before, can also be a great way to get help.

☐ **Waiting for your team to get you to $2000/month** - Believe it or not, it is up to YOU to get to $2000/month, not your team. I can't tell you how many times I have heard, "I would be making $2000/month by now, but my leaders just aren't working it." Unfortunately, you are probably managing them by telling them what to do instead of leading them. Leadership involves inspiring them to want to build their businesses to achieve their personal goals. In truth, managing is all about your desires and not theirs. As mentioned previously, you are building an all-volunteer army of distributors and customers. Find out what they want and be the inspiration to help them manifest it. Also remember that since your business is built of an all-volunteer army, people may come and go, so if all else fails, you can always build another leg or two.

☐ **Relationship challenges with upline** - Okay, here's a tough one. Sometimes before you know how to relate to people with different social styles, you may not know how to connect and develop a relationship with your upline or downline. At the same time, perhaps they haven't learned how to connect with you. If you want to make the relationship work, you will need to learn how to connect better and motivate others. I teach an "Understanding Social

Styles" lesson in week 1 of my course. You can google around for other options. I don't recommend spending time memorizing elements from *Briggs–Myers, Gallop www.Strengthsfinder.com,* and some of the different personality styles assessments. They are too complicated and not what you need because they take too long to figure out. Learn how to find someone's social style within ten to twenty seconds, and it will help you to bridge the gap with them more quickly.

☐ **You are feeling too much pressure to succeed** -Sometimes it comes from your leaders, and sometimes it is internally generated. In both cases, you need to take a breath and take time to smell the roses or some nice calming essential oils. Also, reach upward to find a leader who is a calming force, not someone who is pushing and expecting you to help achieve their results. Hey, we are all human, and personal growth is the number one best result of building your business to $2000/month, Diamond and beyond. When you get there, you will be a better version of yourself, guaranteed. They will be too!

Multiple Training Systems

There are many paths you can travel to reach the $2000/month level. Some focus on direct product sales, some concentrate on internet marketing, others focus on more traditional MLM techniques of dream building, and some are a hybrid of these paths. The approach you take depends mostly on who brought you into this business and what they recommend doing to achieve success.

Unfortunately, some new distributors are sponsored by other distributors who are separated by many levels from distributors who have reached the higher ranks and who have the experience you can lean on to steer you clear of the inevitable challenges that will come your way. A few successful distributors who have reached Diamond or above have developed various courses. But some training programs have been developed by outside companies who have no direct experience building a network marketing business. The experience of some of the creators of these training programs are from traditional sales organizations, and they tend to promote a more traditional (aggressive) approach to prospecting. They focus on sales at all costs, which is useful if you are a dynamic distributor, but which can also leave you feeling uncomfortable while you are prospecting.

In contrast, I prefer to teach business-building information, tools, and "icky-free" prospecting skills that leverage the essential products so you can develop belief and confidence to quickly achieve the goal of $2000/month and above.

I recommend you pick a course that fits your time, budget, and social style. Realize also that some upline sponsors have firm opinions on which program is best. Unfortunately, I have consoled downline members who were in tears because they felt pressured to join expensive leadership training courses that were too advanced and too expensive for them. It's your time and your money, so make choosing a particular training course a choice you can live with.

Do your research, ask questions, and get referrals. In the end, you have to resonate with the program you choose. It has to fit *your* goals and *your* budget.

The good news is that if your chosen course doesn't work for you, there are still plenty of other options. Don't give up! There's more than one way to get to $2000/month!

Point Awareness and Tracking

If you want to build quickly, download a rank worksheet from your company and manually fill it in each week of each month. You will only know how well you are doing if you can plan and track the results.

Most courses will have a weekly planning worksheet you can download. If you are on a weekly coaching or mentoring call with your sponsor, make sure to email your completed form before the call so your coach can help you with any challenges you are having at that time. The more time they have to review it, the better their help can be.

CHAPTER 6

Secret #4: Prioritize Your Time

Your time is your most valuable resource. Unlike money, property, or even relationships, if you lose time, you can't ever get it back or rebuild it. It is just gone.

Sadly, most people treat time with little respect. I am guilty of that too, and even with all my time awareness tools and tricks, I still find myself wasting my valuable time.

These days, I realize that some of my "wasted" time is rejuvenation time, so I don't burn out. So, not all wasted time is truly lost.

That said, as I work with prospects and people in my business, I can see them wasting enormous amounts of time that, if leveraged effectively, could deliver them from the tight financial situations they are in and could create a much better future for them and their families.

How do we become aware of time? My first little exercise will show you the value of even five minutes.

Ready to get started? You will need five minutes of uninterrupted time with NO distractions for this exercise.

Five Minutes Is a Long Time

The good news for the "always busy" people of the world is that you can build much of your MLM business in five-minute chunks of time.

True, it can be built faster if you have larger blocks of time, but you can still get a lot done in five minutes. Let's get started.

- ☐ **Step 1**: Get away from all distractions. (Go outside or hide in a closet if you must.) Put your cell phone in airplane mode. Please do it. The odds of someone you know dying because they couldn't reach you for five minutes is pretty small, and this is an important exercise. Besides, you can check when you are done.
- ☐ **Step 2**: Start your mobile phone clock or timer app or find a kitchen timer and set it for five minutes.
- ☐ **Step 3**: Find a blank wall or someplace away from where you usually study or work.
- ☐ **Step 4**: Stare at the wall and start your timer.
- ☐ **Step 5**: Don't think about anything. Just stare and wait for the ding or beep indicating that five minutes has expired. If you can't stand to trust that the timer will ring, you can take ONE look after you have started it. Don't watch the countdown. That will defeat the purpose. Just wait for the end of time signal.

You will probably find your mind thinking about all kinds of things you need to do or could do or forgot to do, etc. That's okay. This isn't meditation. If you have to write something down because it is extremely important, go ahead, but you have to reset the clock for five minutes and start over.

☐ **Step 6**: Did it seem like a long time? Did you think about all the things you could have been doing? Were you annoyed that you were "wasting" time on this dumb exercise?

Did you realize how LONG five minutes could be? Can you think of things you could do for five minutes that would help to build your business?

Let's explore that a bit. Here's a list of some MLM business activities I came up with. Check the ones that you could do.

○ Send a text message or blitz to friends about something business-related

○ Send a quick email to reconnect with an old friend you were interested in prospecting

○ Do a follow-up call for a one-on-one with a prospect

○ Read another section of this book

○ Look up the use of a product that a prospect was curious about

○ Spend the time rejuvenating with a little meditation

○ Download Zoom to your computer or phone so you can connect with upline or downline on video

○ Check your back office to see if you are tracking against your goal in your business

○ Update your paper prospect tracking sheet with some new information that came in

○ Check how you are doing against the weekly plan you set up on Monday

○ Take a look at the compensation plan to see how one of the bonuses works

○ Look at the town meeting hall or local convention center agenda to see if there are any events coming that you could attend for prospecting purposes

○ Make a list of five people you will connect with today

○ Call one of your team members to let them know you are thinking about them – no business, just check in to see how life is going

○ Download the latest product price list and print it out, so you have a current list available when you need it

○ Look at the current price list you downloaded to get a general idea of prices and products available

○ Print out a few weekly planning sheets and predate them for this or next month

○ Send a text, email, or voice message to an upline leader and ask to connect with them about your business-building goals

○ Get dressed if you are in your PJs and haven't started your day yet. Yes, the five-minute time frame will require some of you to move quickly!

○ Put on makeup or shave if you haven't done it yet. It will make you feel better

○ Install a training app on your smartphone so you can be ready to listen to a free lesson or call.

○ Add a friend to your *SimpleConnector* app and select the "Made a cool friend" campaign and some notes.

○ Open your *SimpleConnector* app and take care of the top task for the day

○ Take a quick five-minute break. Maybe walk outside to the mailbox and back to see if your product package arrived today.

The above list took about fifteen minutes to make and is just what popped into my head. I'm sure there are many other things you can add.

☐ **Step 7:** For the final step, take five additional minutes and create your own list of things you could do in five minutes to build your business. Don't simply copy what I did. Come up with your own stuff first and then use stuff above if you want to fill in the blank lines below. Keep them short. You might want to take a photo of the list or even type and print them (although that might take more than five minutes!).

1. _____

2. _____

3. _____

4. _____

5. _____

The reason I suggested printing the list is because you can take the printed list and put it in your purse, wallet, pocket, or planner. The next time you find yourself with five minutes, take a look at your crunched up little list and do one of the tasks. Your business will grow a little more every time you do it, and you will finally be using those short five-minute blocks of time effectively toward your future. You can also print a few copies and put them up in places you will be. Examples might include: the refrigerator, bathroom mirror, home phone (if you still have one), steering wheel of your car, front door, just any place in your world that you frequent.

Plan Your Week

Do you want to know a secret that rich people know? They plan their time— or pay someone else to do it for them. *Plan your work and then work your plan* is another useful adage.

Do you know what results you will accomplish this week?

If you take a little time early each week to decide on the results you want and then decide on the activities required to get them done, you will be way more ahead than if you don't.

> *The reason we tend to waste a lot of time is because we have not "pre-decided" how we will use it when we have it.*

Another fun thought exercise is to remember how effective and efficient you are the day before you take a long trip or vacation. I bet you plan every hour to get stuff done before you leave. If you don't, you most assuredly will forget to do or bring some necessary things.

The last time you traveled, did you make a checklist of all the things to do and bring? You were probably planning on steroids, just for a day. So, you know how effective planning can be. Imagine how much more you could get done if you prioritized your time and activities each week at the beginning of the week.

The tough thing is that planning is not a natural or even fun thing to do, most of the time — especially if it has to do with work or business building. However, I guarantee that if you do not do it, you WILL lose valuable time. By planning your time, you will increase your chance of building a stable and profitable business and creating the life you deserve.

Here are some tips on how to plan your weeks:

- ☐ Plan your week at the same time each week.
- ☐ Schedule your weekly planning time on your calendar.
- ☐ Use a weekly planning worksheet for a template so you have something to refer to during the week to keep you on track.

I have a weekly planning worksheet I use with my leaders and students in one of my courses. This worksheet is results-based because after taking an $8000 coaching program, I learned that focusing on activities does not guarantee results. What are we after? Results, not just a bunch of busywork.

Result vs. Activity Goals

If I tell you to go out and make two contacts a day, it won't guarantee that any specific results will come of it. However, if we work together and decide ahead of time what results you want for the week, then we can figure out what types of activities will guarantee you get those results. Decide on realistic outcomes.

Simply stating you want to go Diamond this week having enrolled in your MLM last week would be a pretty tight goal, yes? It would not be impossible, though, if we came up with activities that could manifest it.

For example, if you are a major public figure with millions of followers and you told them they would be able to connect directly with you if they joined your MLM business on your team, you could probably hit Diamond in a single day. True, it's not very duplicable, but it WOULD be possible.

Again, decide on the results, and then figure out what activities are required to get there.

The worksheet I created includes the following sections:

➤ Last week's positives and progress, why it matters, and what's next.

➤ A daily habit tracking section for one of your new habits.

➤ A mini reward you will receive if you accomplish your target result for the week.

➤ The amount of time you will allocate each day for each of your activity types (business building, business support, and rejuvenation).

➤ A list of the SMART RESULTS™ you are after this week.

➤ A list of the activities you will do for the chosen results.

➤ Your top ten prospects and each stage they are at.

Make sure to block out the allocated time on your calendar for each of the activities you have listed. It should take about fifteen to thirty minutes to fill it out each Sunday or Monday morning, and it will give you clarity of how to use your time during the week. Don't forget to schedule *this* planning time, too!

In my online training program, we have weekly Monday morning "Planning your Week" Zoom calls where we take one volunteer each week through the process of planning the week, and everyone else fills out their worksheets along with us.

Consider doing something like this with your team. Also, consider working with one of your upline or crossline distributors to create some accountability with each other.

To summarize, simply telling someone to go out and make two contacts a day doesn't guarantee results for the week. If you focus on results, then the activities you do are the variable that can be modified until you get the results you are after. For example: Focus on adding 500 new points in your business this week, not the number of product classes. Why? Because you may have nobody show up to your classes.

Moreover, results are what lead you along the path to whatever rank you desire right now. Results are measurable. Make sense?

Honoring Your Time

One especially important topic is that you need to learn to honor your allocated and scheduled time. Do not let others take over your time blocks. If you allow that, you will not get it done, and your results will suffer. Make deals with people, including your kids, friends, and significant others, that you will not be disturbed at set times on the day so the interfering stops. But don't forget to re-schedule all of these important people back into your life too!

The Multitasking Myth

Okay, here goes my old guy, sexist statement: women indeed tend to be better at multitasking than guys. However, it is true that nobody can truly multitask, not even women.

Traditionally, guys find it easy to hyper-focus on only one thing at a time, much to the amazement of the women in their lives. (How DOES a guy mindlessly watch TV for hours? Check out Mark Gungor's YouTube video for a funny explanation called *Tale of Two Brains.* You will be laughing on the floor in no time.)

https://youtu.be/29JPnJSmDs0

Sure, there are multiple tasks you have to do that don't require focus, like doing the laundry, watching TV, and cooking a roast all at them same time, then you can do them. However, only one of those tasks gets the primary focus at any given time.

Multitasking is switching between tasks moment to moment. For example, when the dryer buzzes, you wait for a commercial, dash to the dryer, grab the clothes, and start folding them. Then the TV show pops back on, all with a roast in the oven.

When the roast timer dings, you do the same thing. You'd probably lay out the clothes, so they don't wrinkle, dash to the kitchen to turn off the oven, and then return to folding and TV.

All of the tasks gets done seemingly simultaneously, but the truth is you are stopping and starting each as priorities changes.

This is fine if you are doing tasks that don't require you to be 100 percent at the moment, like follow-up calls, one-on-ones, planning your week, studying how you get paid, listening to instructors, and other mundane but necessary business activities.

When you are focusing your brain on these more complex types of tasks and you pop off the topic for even one minute, it can take many minutes to get back on track. Sometimes you never get back on track, so it is critical NOT to get distracted in the first place.

Also, there is nothing more frustrating than talking to people and having them always "put you on hold" or try to do other things while they are talking to you. You feel like you are not valued, so you want to end the conversation. This is NOT the way to BUILD or even maintain an existing relationship.

So, where am I going with this?

If you allocate time for a given "thinking" or "relationship-building" task, do not let it get interrupted. Make deals with people to have the time you need to get the high-priority task done.

Manage Your Distractions

Have you ever gotten to the end of a day, week, month, or year, and wondered where all your time had gone?

Time management isn't about managing time; it's about managing priorities. Both the wealthiest and most impoverished people on the planet have the same twenty-four hours in a day. It's what you do with those twenty-four hours that will determine if you are successful or not.

> *Time management isn't about managing time.*
> *It's about managing priorities.*

Do you control your time? Or does it control you?

This section is about how to handle distractions: all those little time sucks that occur all day long. Examples include:

➤ Telephone rings, you pick it up.

➤ "You've got mail" or "ding" . . . you see it.

➤ "Click-click" . . . you check your text.

➤ "Be-bop" . . . you check your Facebook Messenger.

➤ Baby cries and you drop what you're doing to figure out what they need.

➤ A conversation in the next cubicle draws your attention.

➤ A favorite TV show comes on, and you stop to watch it.

➤ Your spouse or kids come into the room with some "emergency" that must be handled by you, RIGHT NOW!

What things distract you regularly? List them below:

1. _____

2. _____

3. _____

4. _____

In every example above, you have put someone else's priorities ABOVE YOUR OWN! Think about that. YOU have pre-decided to allow these distractions to happen! You have given them ALL permission to be MORE IMPORTANT than the task you are trying to complete.

Do you want to have a better life? If so, then it is time to take charge of your time priorities. Imagine how much more productive you could be if you stayed IN THE ZONE to finish the task.

The good news is that it is easier than you think. You can CHOOSE to control your life's distractions. For example, you can:

O Turn off the phone ringer (no buzz-mode, either!) or use the "Do Not Disturb" mode on home and mobile phones.

O Turn off email notifications in settings or airplane mode.

O Turn off text notifications in settings or airplane mode.

O Get a babysitter or trade time with friends to share kid-sitting during "MLM business office hours".

O Use a headset with study music or use the Focus@Will app when you need to concentrate.

O Use white noise to block out distractions.

○ Set your DVR to capture movies you want to watch so you can CHOOSE when to watch them.

○ Tell interrupters, "Please talk to the second-in-command to get problems solved during my MLM-biz office hours". (LATER, make time up to them by doing predetermined and agreed-to fun activities).

Are you feeling withdrawal symptoms cutting everything off? Maybe start with one at a time or try a new one every three days or so — NOT!

REALLY? Did you think I would let you get off this easily?

NO WAY! I thought you wanted to build your business quickly! How bad do you want it?

DO ALL OF THEM and see if you survive!

Who knows, you might break some bad habits and magically come up with the time you crave to reach your targeted rank or income level. By the way, this process happens at every rank – even intergalactic super Diamond. Those lost seconds add up to minutes, hours, days, and years of lost productivity.

Do you want change in your life? **THEN CHANGE!** The most successful people in the world manage their time priorities or PAY someone else to do it for them! One thing for sure: they had to do it themselves before they could afford to pay someone else to help them.

What have you got to lose? You can always go back to your comfort zone and not change anything in your life. But that's the topic for another chapter!

Do you want change in your life? Then Change!

CHAPTER 7

Secret #5:
Your SMART WHY Is Your Fuel

I f you have been around the Multi-Level Marketing (MLM) industry for even a month or more, you'll hear this everywhere: "You need a WHY to build a successful business." Moreover, just so we are clear, your WHY is your motivating force or fuel to move you out of your comfort zone and into your zone of productivity so you can change your life.

It is the one thing that will motivate you to get off your butt when you don't feel like it to go out to prospect or to present in front of a group of people (or even to finish reading or listening to this book) when you would rather watch TV, spend time on Facebook, or go dancing.

The truth is, most people have no clue how to figure out their WHY, let alone the WHY of others. A WHY is an elusive little creature! Why? Because most people figure it is some major life purpose or grand design for why you are on this planet. Others think it is just some cool thing like traveling, buying a home on the coast, or quitting your job.

Just know that your WHY is a very personal thing that can't be generalized. Also, if your WHY doesn't change your behavior and get you out of your comfort zone, it is useless to help you build your business. I know this is harsh, but I'm not here to sugarcoat things. I want you to be successful, so let's help you figure out a WHY that works for you!

Why Your WHY Didn't Help You

Here's a common scenario. All the experts told you to figure out your WHY, and some even gave you a simple five- to fifteen-minute exercise to find it. You wrote it down on paper, and it felt good that you could visualize the reason to build your business. Then, you started building your business but found you were not moving along as well as you had expected.

You had challenges, of course, like everyone else, with life getting in the way of your progress. Stuff like taking the kids to school, driving them to soccer practice several times a week, spending a few weeks getting ready for the Easter party, and reserving a summer vacation in June or July to keep your sanity. Then there's shopping for new clothes and school supplies in August for the kids, and of course the few weeks in November and December preparing for Thanksgiving and Christmas. Moreover, you cook, clean, do the laundry, get groceries, take care of your significant other, and a lot of other things. I get it: You're busy!

You may have joined your MLM company because it seemed like an excellent way to build a business centered around those products. They said it would only take a short amount of time to share them with your friends and you could grow a nice little business. Moreover, they were right: you did grow a nice

LITTLE business. However, is a LITTLE business what you wanted? Probably not.

You were probably hoping for more than that. You have seen the ultra-successful Diamonds with their lifestyles and said, "Why not me? I want that too!" Never mind the fact that they look like they were made to do this business. They were perfect and living the dream, unlike you. You might have thought, "How can I have that, too, because my life sucks." You probably wanted more than what you have now.

Did you know that every one of those polished Diamonds looked a lot more like you when they started than they do now? But then they discovered and leveraged their WHY. It was a big part of how they got to Diamond. I always say nobody goes Diamond by accident. It takes a lot of hard work.

What if all you want to do is make a few thousand dollars a month? You still need a WHY because going from nothing to $2000/month is harder than going from $2000/month to Diamond. At least at $2K/month, you have proven you know how to prospect and structure your team. It turns out that all rank increases need a good WHY or you will stay where you are, or worse, drop down in rank.

If this has already happened to you, what went wrong? Simple. Your WHY wasn't strong enough to change your priorities and behavior daily. If your WHY does not cause you to wake up thinking, "What one thing do I need to do today to get the results I have set this week?" then you will quickly sink back into your old habits. You need a more effective WHY: one that will cause you to change your habits and priorities daily.

Let's dig into some of the common WHY issues.

Your Dreams *vs.* An *Effective* WHY

Most so-called experts teach only a surface-level approach to finding a WHY. A life purpose, a dream, and knowing your destiny are beautiful things, but they don't motivate you daily, and I can prove it to you.

Let's say your dream is to own a second home on the Oregon coast or a nice tropical island away from your snowy winters. Sound nice? Great. Let's see how this is a useless WHY to motivate you to change your daily habit. I'm going to start with some questions.

- ✓ When do you want to achieve this? Next month? Two years from now? Five years from now?
- ✓ How much will it cost? $20,000? $205,000? $520,000? $2,040,000?

Okay, let's say you figure it out: You want to buy it on October 1, 2025, for $625,000, and you need $200,000 down to buy it. (It's an extremely tiny island!)

Let's say that today is October 1, 2020. That leaves you five years to pull it off, and you calculate you'll need to earn an extra $3,333 per month to cover the down payment. That's a stable business builder rank, so you start planning it all out and figure you'll be able to earn less money now and more money later as your business grows. All is great. Let's say this month's portion will be $500. That works out to about $125/week, or $25/day. You've got this! So, off you go on your plan, and you're doing great for a couple of days. You're out talking to people and sell-ing your products. But then you find out you won an all expenses paid trip to Hawaii for two that leaves in four days.

Do you decide to skip a week of business-building time for this free trip? Heck, it's only a week, and your boss gave you time off work. Besides, you're certain you can make it up later, so you say, "Sure! Let's go!"

Of course, it takes a couple of days to prepare for the trip and then, upon return, another four days off to catch up. The total of time you've lost is reaching a couple of weeks. Now you have to make up the money you lost by the missed MLM biz-building workdays. Let's see, that's about half a month, so you'll need to make $50/day. Hmmm, it is harder, but still doable. Then, your kids say, "Mom! You promised to take me to the mall to shop for new clothes!" or "Dad! You promised to take me to the big game!" You feel guilty that you went to Hawaii and missed time with your kids, and so you put off work for the mall or the game to be with your them. Then it happens again over the next cou-ple of weeks, with more activities like school plays and parent meetings, and now you're up to $75/day. Next you decide to ad-just your monthly goals, so you don't need as much per week.

It has only been a month or so after you first came up with your WHY and your plan for how you'll get it, but already you're starting to change it. How long did it take for you to change your priorities completely? But, you say, "No big deal. The goal was five years from now, a few weeks won't make a difference."

Are you starting to see what's happening? Your WHY didn't help you with your daily habits. You are just pushing off things like usual, and you didn't change anything with that WHY.

In reality, it was just a dream, not a powerful WHY. If your WHY doesn't motivate you daily, it is not strong enough.

A Powerful WHY

Here is another example. Let's say I asked, "Could you sell two product starter kits ($500 each) in the next four days to new prospects?" Do you believe you would (or even could) do that? I'm guessing probably not.

Okay, now let's say I explained that your life purpose, your dream, or your destiny would take three months longer to accomplish if you didn't sell two $500 starter kits in the next four days to new prospects. Do you believe you would go out and do that? I'm still guessing probably not.

So, let's change things up. What if I told you your kid, mom, sister, partner (pick someone you love) was gravely ill and needed money right now for a life-saving procedure, and I explained that your loved one wouldn't survive more than a week if you didn't enroll two people with $500 starter kits within those four days to get them that procedure. Do you think you would figure out a way to make it happen? Did you feel it in your gut? Did you realize suddenly that EVERY MINUTE OF EVERY DAY MATTERED? Did you notice that your WHY suddenly got so powerful it would cause you to get out of your comfort zone and make it happen, no matter what?

Here is the funny thing, though: did anything really change? The time frame to sell those $500 starter kits is the same, but your emotions took over and drove you to action. <u>Your heart took charge over your mind</u>. That is what a powerful, motivating WHY looks like. By not having a strong WHY, you are wasting your TIME. You can do anything with the right mental and emotional kick in the butt, and that is what a powerful WHY does. It gives you the drive to do what needs to get done despite life's challenges and distractions

It's time for you to get your powerful, motivating WHY figured out if you want to build this business fast. Don't stop short of finding your REAL WHY.

Your S.M.A.R.T. WHY™

Have you ever heard of S.M.A.R.T. goals? Converting regular goals into SMART goals provides more clarity and makes them more believable. I'll go through the letters of the acronym using the simple example of a goal of making your car payments with network marketing income.

The letters of the SMART acronym represent:

- ➤ **S** - Specific - A clear decision of what you want to accomplish. An example might be "Make my car payments with my MLM income."
- ➤ **M** - Measurable - A numeric value that, when reached, shows you can hit the goal. For example, "Make $278.00/month for a car payment."

➤ **A** - Achievable - Is this goal something you believe you can do? For example, if you get to a rank in your business where you earn $300 to $500 per month, you could use $278.00 of your earnings for your car payment. Do you believe you could hit that rank in two months?

➤ **R** - Relevant - Is this something you want to do? If you hit the $500/month rank, how would it feel to be able to pay for your car using MLM business income? Would it free up money to do other things? Would you want this?

➤ **T** - Time-bound - When do you want to accomplish this goal? For example, "Start making payments in 2 months."

So, putting it all together: "*Within two months I will start making my $278.00 car payments with my network marketing business income, which will free up that much money for other things I want (or need) to do.*" Do you see how this is much more powerful than merely, "I want to use my MLM biz income to make my car payments"?

A few years ago, I had an epiphany of creating SMART WHYs to help get the same sort of clarity. Here's how it works.

USE PENCIL SO YOU CAN UPDATE IT LATER!!! (Fill in the form below as you go through the five steps below.)

(**S**)pecific   _____

(**M**)easurable   _____

(**A**)chievable   _____

(**R**)elevent   _____

(**T**)ime-bound   _____

Now let's go through the process of filling out the SMART WHY worksheet:

☐ **STEP 1**: **(T)**ime-bound - Let's start with the **T**. Fill in a time of either one or two months. It will help to create some urgency with whatever choice you make for your goal. You can hone this after you have filled in the **S** and **M** lines.

☐ **STEP 2**: **(S)**pecific - Come up with something you want that is important to you that you would love to pay for using your MLM business income within the timeframe chosen in step 1. Examples might include:

○ Music lessons for your child once a week

○ Trip to Disneyland with your kids and partner

○ A weekly maid to clean your home

○ A biweekly maid to do the laundry every few days

○ Money to put into savings

○ Car payments or a new car

○ Money to donate to charity

○ House payments

○ Tickets for your team for a special night out

Brainstorm some of your ideas below:

1. _____

2. _____

3. _____

4. _____

A few rules: Make sure you really want it. Make sure to calculate the cost within $50 or so (spend the time to research the actual price if you don't already know it). Fill in your choice next to **S**.

☐ **STEP 3: (M)**easurable - Decide how much you will spend out of your MLM income for your chosen goal: **S**. You won't know what that exact income will be yet, but for your SMART WHY to be believable, you get to look at your current income and project out a couple of months. See below for examples for **M**.

Here's the tricky part. If you are too conservative, it won't work. You won't have any incentive to work harder. However, if it is too crazy high and you are not close as the date approaches, then you won't believe it, and you'll give up. Make sure the balance is just right.

Example 1: Let's say you make $200/month in your MLM business and your WHY is a rent payment of $800/month. That's a difference of $600. So, you would enter "$600 more per month" for **M**. You have two months to get there, so don't make it too easy. You could put in "$800 per month" if you want to hit a higher goal.

Example 2: If your current MLM business income is $2700/month and you want to be at $6000/month, then enter "$3300 per month" into **M**. Remember, you have two months to get there, so don't make it too easy. If you want to challenge yourself, enter a harder value into **M**.

☐ **STEP 4: (R)elevent** - Look at what you wrote in for the **S**. Tap into your heart, and see if you REALLY WANT IT. If not, stop and pick something else. Take your time going back and forth between **S** and **R** until you're really committed. Write "YES" next to **R** once you figure it out.

☐ **STEP 5: (A)chievable** - Okay, you're on the home stretch. Do you believe you can do this with the help of your team and tools you're learning in this book or training program you have joined? Have you calculated how much more you would have to make each week to pull this off? For example, if your target is $400 in two months, then that's an extra average income increase of $50 per week ($400 divided by two months). Note that in this type of business, you will be making more in the second month than in the first, so in your first week you might only need to make an extra $25, knowing you'll be bringing in maybe an extra $75 per week as the second month approaches. If you can believe the numbers are doable, then write "YES" next to the **A**. Remember, stretch yourself so you'll grow your business.

Now, take a step back and look at your **S** again. How badly do you want it? Remember, if it doesn't do much for you, it won't motivate you daily.

If you are struggling with the **S**, you are probably someone who likes to help others more than yourself. Try to find something you could be a part of that would make a real difference to someone (e.g., taking a brief trip with a loved one for a getaway weekend; helping someone pay for a wish-list item;

buying a fun gift or reward for the winners of an incentive award; or planning a special event for your team). Make sure they know you will pay for it with your MLM business income. That will add more power to the S. Also, you'll have to be accountable to them, so you'll try harder, which will help you. How do you feel about your selected WHY?

☐ Does it make you smile?

☐ Do you feel a little nervous about accomplishing it?

☐ Have you chosen someone as an accountability partner or partial recipient of the reward?

☐ Do you believe if you worked hard (and smart), you could pull it off?

☐ Is it specific?

☐ Would you feel a little nervous about posting your journey with your team?

☐ Would it inspire your team to root for you or even come up with their own plans?

☐ Do you think it would cause you to put your MLM business into your day as a priority and wake up with an extra bounce in your step if you accomplished it?

☐ Can you see how a powerful WHY can affect your daily habits and cause you to go the extra mile for your goals?

Hopefully, all the above answers are "yes." If so, you are well on your way to having a power WHY to help you build your business over the next couple of months. Repeat these steps again as you near the end of the second month to prepare for the next couple of months.

Your WHY will be continually evolving as you build your business. If you don't regularly update your WHY, your business will stagnate and may even start to dissipate.

CHAPTER 8

Secret #6:
Comfort Stops Progress

D o you have everything you want in life? Time? Money? Relationships? Body? Skills? Stuff? Talents? Energy? Knowledge? Spiritual connections? Anything else come to mind?

If your answer to all the above is "yes," then you can pretty much stop reading this book about building a successful network marketing business and relax. Get comfortable in your big easy chair, kick your shoes off, watch a movie, and enjoy your life.

Of course, the truth is that nobody has everything. Everyone from the richest to the poorest and the youngest to the oldest wants something they don't already possess.

Unfortunately, just wanting something different often isn't enough to get it; this is especially true if that something is a lot different than what we already have. Why? Because people also like to be comfortable. It's just human nature. Change is hard, so we tend to put it off for another day. Countless self-improvement programs are purchased and not consumed. Often, we read the first pages of a book or listen to the first half hour of an audio or video recording. I have seen this repeatedly. I'm in the world of self-improvement, and even I haven't listened to programs that I purchased with good money. *I also know that the percentage of people who get this far in this book is scary-low.*

This is sad because the process of personal growth helps us create a better version of ourselves. Have you ever known anyone who joined an MLM either in your past or recently? Have you watched them as they grew in rank to Diamond? They are different after a while, aren't they? Aside from the genuinely nice passive income, their confidence and aura are different. People want to be around them! Odds are they weren't like that when they joined the MLM company. They struggled, just like you, to find the secret sauce to get them to Diamond. But they had something that most people don't have: a clear and powerfully motivating WHY, along with the tenacity of not letting anything stop them.

Looking inward, what is stopping *you?* Is it a lack of money, knowledge, perfect body, time, or something else? This killer of progress is called *limiting beliefs.* Not believing you can do something will stop you every time. Your confidence suffers. You let yourself get distracted. You spend your money on stuff that won't help you progress toward the goals you have set, and then you put other plans ahead of your business.

The rest of this chapter is here to give you some guidance on how to get COMFORTABLE being UNCOMFORTABLE and how to identify some of your limiting beliefs so you can push past them to the greatness you are now and deserve in the future.

Time to Get Uncomfortable

The reality is that change is hard, but it is essential for personal growth, both emotionally and financially. I tell people, "Personal growth sucks! However, the results are amazing." The best thing about reaching your goals in your MLM is that after you have pushed through the tough stuff, you have become a better version of yourself. It's true. I've seen it many times.

Think back to when someone you know first started in your MLM. They probably fumbled around until things started sticking. Strongly driven people sometimes even tick people off because of the way they push. Then a funny thing happens. They begin to realize that this is a RELATIONSHIP-business. They learn that they will have a successful business only if they help others find their WHY and create freedoms in their lives through their own successful business. After a while, they become the coolest people you know because they have experienced personal growth and have become that better version of themselves.

Another example is on the opposite end of the spectrum. Maybe you know someone who started out caring more about everyone else than themselves and gave all their samples away. They practically went broke because they gave away so much product. Unfortunately, they weren't making any real money. Only when they realized that this is a relationship-BUSINESS were they able to push past the discomfort and ask their prospects if they would instead buy it at retail or wholesale. It seemed a little awkward at first, but then they tried it out.

Everything started to change, and people started signing up. They finally had a business.

In both cases, the person had to get a little uncomfortable first, and then it became easy and more natural.

Here's a good one. If you think about all the defining moments of your life, you will realize they were first uncomfortable. Examples include:

☐ Your first kiss

☐ Your first day of high school

☐ The first time you merged into fast-moving traffic

☐ The first time you held a baby

☐ The first time you asked someone out for a date

☐ The first time you started a job

Can you think of any other examples in your life? List a few:

_____

_____

_____

_____

_____

_____

_____

In each of the above examples, you were initially uncomfortable. However, after you did them a few times, they were no longer uncomfortable, were they?

If you want your business to grow, you are going to have to do something different, something uncomfortable. But if you do it a few more times, it will begin to be natural to you, and after a while, it might even become fun.

Trust me, you will LOVE the new you if you get off the cushy, comfortable chair. Besides, if you do it right, you can buy a much nicer chair later — in your new house overlooking the ocean or lake!

Limiting Beliefs

Did you know you have limiting beliefs? You have preconceived ideas of:

- ☐ What YOU are worth
- ☐ How much your TIME is worth
- ☐ How long you will live
- ☐ If you deserve success
- ☐ If you deserve happiness
- ☐ What people think about you
- ☐ How much money you should make
- ☐ How much success you can handle
- ☐ If you are pretty or handsome enough
- ☐ If you are smart enough
- ☐ If you are too tall or too short
- ☐ If you are too fat or too skinny
- ☐ If your skin color will limit your success
- ☐ If your religion will interfere with your business
- ☐ If your gender is impacting how much you make

I could go on and on. Can you think of limiting beliefs you might want to push past? Write them down below and then think about them.

_____

_____

_____

_____

_____

_____

Did nothing come to mind? If so, you might not think you have them. That's fine. Let's test that theory.

Do you believe you could make $500/month in your network marketing business? I want you to think about it. Consider your experience so far making money in your MLM business. Yes? Great, let's go on.

Do you believe you could make $5000/month in your network marketing business? I want you to think about it. Consider your experience so far making money in your company. Yes? Great, let's go on.

Do you believe you could make $50,000/month in your MLM business? I want you to think about it. Consider your experience so far making money in your business. Yes? Great, let's go on.

Do you believe you could make $500,000/month in your MLM business? I want you to think about it. Consider your experience so far making money in your business.

When doing this exercise, most people get stuck somewhere between $5,000/month and $50,000/month. The reason is that they have a limiting belief of how much THEY could personally make. They know others have done it, but they don't think *they* could do it.

What if I told you there are people making millions per month in network marketing? There are! Moreover, I guarantee that these same people didn't believe they would be making that much when they started. They PUSHED PAST their limiting beliefs and made it happen.

You can push past any limiting belief you have. Did you notice the too short, too tall, too fat, too skinny ones in the examples? We all feel we have flaws, whether we want to admit to them or not and whether we want to acknowledge how they impact our decisions in life or not.

One of the most uncomfortable exercises I have ever done involved standing in a circle of people who all sat down and described me. Even though they were all strangers, they figured me out to a T. That's when I stopped pretending to be someone I wasn't. It didn't matter. Everyone surrounding me saw right through it, and it was liberating for me not to have to worry about it anymore.

The sooner you get past your limiting beliefs, the faster you will grow your business, and the better your life will be. The new, improved YOU will be worth the growing pains. I promise.

CHAPTER 9

Secret #7:
Transform Fear Into Confidence

It is incredible how much our fears can hold us back from success. Fear is on a sliding scale, and it is very personal. What scares one person is often a passion for someone else. Examples include:

> ➤ Fear of height vs. skydivers
> ➤ Fear of public speaking vs. politicians or performers (not much difference in some cases!)
> ➤ Fear of flying vs. hang glider pilots
> ➤ Fear of driving vs. race car drivers

We know, in our head, that we "shouldn't" be afraid, but there it is: a flashing red light saying "DANGER" along with that pit in our stomach that holds us back from our greatness.

My biggest fear has always been public speaking. Even presenting in front of three of my leaders used to cause me to shake. I had to have a PowerPoint I could read in front of them, or I would cancel the event. It would take me hours to prepare the "perfect" PowerPoint. Fortunately, I can now get in front of hundreds without panic and fear (and even without a PowerPoint)!

Over the past few years, I have hosted more than 1,000 Zoom video calls with my students and downline, and I have no fear of doing it anymore. Not true on the first bunch of calls, however. Eight years ago, I struggled even to do voice-only conference phone calls. What changed? For me, it was just getting uncomfortable and doing it. I had gone Diamond and desperately wanted to be able to share my wisdom and secrets to my team and others. I prepared a great script, set up the call, and let people know about it. (I was greatly tempted not to tell anyone about it so no one would show, but I did it anyway.) My first call had 57 people on it, and I had to take a shower afterward because my anxiety made me sweat so much, but I did it! Whew!

My goal for this chapter is to help you get over some of the fears that may be holding you back. You can also look at the previous chapter, "Comfort Stops Progress," for some other ideas.

Most Fear Is in Our Head

Years ago, I learned an interesting acronym for fear: False Evidence Appearing Real. When you think about it, this makes sense. After all, in my case-fear of public speaking-why was I worried or afraid? What worried me? What was the worst that could happen? I guess people could take shots at me because I told them something they didn't want to hear, but there was no real reason for me to be afraid. It sure FELT real to me, butterflies and all, but the fear wasn't justifiable. Most fears rarely make sense in our modern lives. After all, we don't have sabertooth tigers chasing us in our homes. So, it is all in our head. Our subconscious is trying to protect us, but from what?

Common Distributor Fears

Some common fears of distributors may include: (Check any that might apply to you)

- ☐ Not knowing what to say when someone asks a question
- ☐ Not having the right product when it is needed
- ☐ Not smart enough to understand the compensation plan
- ☐ Not smart enough to build a business
- ☐ Not having a nice enough place to do presentations
- ☐ Not having a nice enough car
- ☐ Being too old or too young
- ☐ Not having enough time to build an MLM business
- ☐ Not having enough friends to prospect
- ☐ Not having enough money to build the business
- ☐ Failure in past attempts at network marketing
- ☐ Not understanding business
- ☐ Not understanding how to use the products
- ☐ Not building fast enough for their upline
- ☐ Not being a leader
- ☐ Not understanding technology
- ☐ Not understanding the full spectrum of the products
- ☐ Saying something that could get them in trouble
- ☐ Not having a computer
- ☐ Not having a smartphone
- ☐ Not having a supportive spouse
- ☐ Not being able to find their WHY
- ☐ Fear of public speaking
- ☐ Failing at giving a class – no attendance, failed demos
- ☐ Building a business and having your company shut down
- ☐ Getting sick from someone else at an event

Are any of yours on the list? This is all I could come up with in ten minutes of typing, but trust me, there are a lot more. What are some of yours? List them here.

_____

_____

_____

_____

_____

_____

Building Confidence

One thing is for sure: if you push through your fear(s), you will become more confident. But how do we do this? The good news is that since fears are not real, all we have to do is push through them knowing they won't really kill us. How do we do that?

Let's pick some of the common fears from the previous section and come up with some possible ways to overcome them.

Not knowing what to say

This fear is widespread, especially for analytical people. They don't want to look like an idiot in front of others. In this case, the solution is pretty simple: memorize a simple script as a response to questions that stump you. Let's say the question is "What product do you use for stress?"

Here are some possible scripts you could memorize ahead of time:

➢ "That's a great question! I'd also like to know the answer to that question. Would it be okay if I call my friend and find out for you?"

➢ "That's a great question. I have an app on my phone that has all that type of information. Would it be okay if I look it up for you?"

➢ "That's a great question. I have a book I use to find that stuff out. Let me show you how to figure this out in case you have questions when I'm not around. Would that be okay with you?"

Memorize one of these scripts and try it out a few times. I'd recommend practicing your script in front of your iPhone video camera and playing it back. Keep doing it until it feels natural in your own words.

Memorizing a script is an example of one way to help you until you are confident enough to improvise on your own. After a while, you won't have any fear when someone asks that type of question.

You should also note that the "what product to use" question is an example of one you should not answer instantly, because if you did it without looking it up, then YOU are the expert. Trust me; if you want your time back, you don't want to be the expert. Show them how to look it up, and you'll empower them to be independent of you. Over time, all your leaders will become independent, and you'll get your time back. Very cool.

Not understanding technology

The best way to control this fear is to become educated about technology to the extent that it no longer scares you. Do you have a smartphone? Can you call from it? Can you send a text? Can you send an email? What else do you need? If you want to log into the back office, call your sponsor or one of your MLM friends and offer to buy them lunch if they'll show you how to log in and move around. Just make sure to tell them to limit their training to the simple stuff and ask them to let you do the typing and mouse clicking so you really get it. Fearful about other issues? This approach is an example of getting help to learn something you don't know so you can start to do it yourself.

Failing at giving a class

If you are fearful of giving a class, then make sure you have someone there the first time who is comfortable giving the class in your place, and then watch them do it for you. Next time do just a little bit of the class. You may want to have notes in your hand or a PowerPoint on the screen or TV. That's okay. Later, do a little bit more of the class. Keep it up until you are doing the entire class. Now, you are the expert, and you will be helping your new people to do the same thing. After a while, they'll think you were a born instructor. (Only you will know where you came from!) This approach is an excellent example of using baby steps to push past your fear.

Building a business only to have your company shut down

This was a fear one of my leaders had a few years ago. I told her, "Do you feel you know more about sales and connecting with people now than you did when you joined our MLM company?" She said, "Yes." Then, I asked her, "If our company disappeared, do you think you could shift your knowledge to another MLM product line?" She said, "Yes." I said, "Then what's the problem? You'll have a little hiccup if you ever need to restart, but you already know what you need to know about selling and connecting." She said, "Your right. Okay. I'm not worried anymore." The problem and her fears were gone.

So, whatever you're fearing, think through the problem and, if necessary, talk to your upline to come up with ideas of how to solve it.

In all the cases I've mentioned, you'll gain more and more confidence as you build your business because you'll either experience these fears yourself or have a downline ask you how to get over it. Remember, you can always read a book or ask an upline leader for some golden advice. You are part of a vast team of people who want you to be successful. Everyone above you for many levels is earning money on your orders, so they owe you some help. Keep going up your leader tree until you find some folks who will help. I'm sure they'll be happy to do so. Just make sure you schedule a time with them, and don't miss the appointment since they are probably busy too! Also, if you are afraid of asking them for help, then think about this: if you had downline distributors, even ten levels down, who needed some helpful advice from you, would you be annoyed and not want them to contact you? Of course not! So, reach out to them.

Handling Prospect Objections

Another common fear is not knowing how to handle an objection from a prospect or someone you respect. Examples of prospect objections that may come up include these:

- ☐ I don't have enough money to buy the kit
- ☐ I don't have enough time to build the business
- ☐ I don't have any friends
- ☐ I couldn't do this MLM business
- ☐ I don't want to join an illegal pyramid

A common approach to handle any of the above is called "Feel, Felt, Found." To apply this approach, simply say these lines:

1. **I know how you feel.**
2. **I felt the same way.**
3. **What I found out is** _____.
4. **Would you like to learn more?**

For example, if they say, "*I don't have money to buy the starter kit*," you would say, "I know how you feel." "I felt the same way." Then fill in line 3 with something like, "What I found out is _You can make enough money in this business to pay for the kit in three months_." Followed by #4, Would you like to learn more (or how)?"

Here are some great responses to the rest of that list of objections.

- ◆ **No Time**: "I build my business in the little five-minute cracks of time I have learned how to find in my life."
- ◆ **No friends**: "The one thing this business does is to help us make new friends. Then, if we like them, we can offer them the business. Do you think you could make new friends by showing them how to make an extra thousand a month in a side business?"
- ◆ **Can't do business**: "Turns out it is more about making friends and then deciding if you would like to work with them. It's cool, and as you become increasingly successful, you'll have lots of new friends."
- ◆ **Illegal Pyramid**: "The good thing is that our company is not an illegal pyramid. Illegal pyramids pay their distributors money they make by signing up other people. We make our money through product flow." (See the glossary for more details).

In all cases, you would follow it up with, "Would you like to know how?"

Can you think of any objections that prospects may have? If so, write them down below and see if you can craft a "Feel, Felt, Found" response.

Objection #1: _____

Response #1: I know how you feel. I felt the same way. Here's what I found:

_____

Objection #2: _____

Response #2: I know how you feel. I felt the same way. Here's what I found:

_____

Objection #3: _____

Response #3: I know how you feel. I felt the same way. Here's what I found:

_____

Objection #4: _____

Response #4: I know how you feel. I felt the same way. Here's what I found:

_____

Objection #5: _____

Response #5: I know how you feel. I felt the same way. Here's what I found:

_____

Objection #6: _____

Response #6: I know how you feel. I felt the same way. Here's what I found:

_____

Hopefully, you are starting to get the hang of it. Just remember to take a deep breath when you feel that pit in your stomach. Step away for a few minutes if you can, and then do something that will help to calm things down. You can do this. You have already conquered so much in your life!

CHAPTER 10

Secret #8:
Practice "Icky-Free" Prospecting

One of my front-line leaders who focuses primarily on selling products says she does this because according to her, "trying to get <u>other people</u> to sell products feels icky." Have you ever felt that way? If so, it is because you are doing it the wrong way! Anytime you feel "icky", it is because you are making it about YOU and not about them! Examples include:

- ☐ Trying to convince family and friends that this MLM is going to work (so they'll support you)
- ☐ Trying to justify the cost of the "expensive" products to people (so they will buy them)
- ☐ Trying to convince buyers to convert from customer to distributor (so you can move them to a better position on your team)
- ☐ Trying to push BOGOs (Buy One, Get One) or product specials to your team (to make a higher bonus this month)

Can you think of anything like this that you are doing? List them below. Remember, awareness is the first step to "recovery"!

Example:

I _push BOGOS_ .

so that _I can qualify for a higher bonus to make more money_ .

1. I _____

so that _____

2. I _____

so that _____

3. I _____

so that _____

4. I _____

so that _____

The icky feeling happens because you have put your priorities over someone else's, and deep-down feel this. In all the above examples, you are trying to convince someone else to buy oils so YOU will make more money. It feels selfish, and that is NOT who you are.

After you have been doing this for a while and start to get a taste of some extra money coming in, you begin to realize it might be possible to quit your job if you commit and go to the next level. Then you discover that the next level means converting customers into distributors. You need to teach them to build their own business and/or have their own account with orders each month. You are pushing them from simply BUYING products to SELLING them too. Deep down, however, you know that you are pushing to sell more (and in turn are pushing your team to do the same) because YOU will make more money, not because THEY asked you to help them make more money to advance in rank.

Unfortunately, many leaders teach this approach because it creates more volume and therefore higher bonuses.

WHAT IF... your focus was to find and help people by asking them what they need and then helping them get it? How could you feel icky?

How could it ever feel bad to help other people who are asking for your help to make their lives better? The problem is that you started the entire conversation selling products instead of trying to help them get what they need. So, what is it they need?

To understand *icky-free prospecting* you get to think at a higher-level, so stick with me on this.

Higher-Level Thinking

Why do people need the products? Usually, especially if you are part of a wellness company, it is to help them solve some health, wellness, or other issue they are having. You say, "Of course; that's obvious!" But what is one of the biggest contributors to their issues?

Stress! Stress tends to trigger many different issues.

When our body is stressed, it starts eating itself from the inside out, creating all these nasty "bugs" that destroy its natural defenses and making it vulnerable to everything from colds and flus, to organs out of balance, all the way to the top of the chain, cancer. We use wellness products to help reduce the stress in our lives, and many times it works — or at least reduces the severity of many of the problems.

But, you say, "Sure, I get this. What's new?" Let's hop up to the next level of thinking. Consider this question: "What is often the highest cause of stress?" Most people will respond with things like:

- ☐ The kids
- ☐ My spouse
- ☐ No time
- ☐ My job
- ☐ My health (this one is a spiral — stress causes your health to suffer, which causes more stress, and down the spiral you go)
- ☐ Not enough money

When you think about it, you probably realize that the lack of money is the granddaddy of them all, because with plenty of money, most of the other stresses are solvable. Here's how that may play out when you have more money on hand.

- ☐ **Kids:** You can have more time to play with them, money for daycare or buying them things they both want and need.
- ☐ **Spouse:** You can have more to play with your partner or money to pay for things to do or have that make your lives more fun.

- ☐ **Time:** With passive (royalty-like) income coming in every month, you can do what you want, when you want.
- ☐ **Job:** With passive (royalty-like) income coming in every month, you can drop-kick that stressful job.
- ☐ **Health:** With an abundance of money, you can reduce your stress, which naturally improves your health, and you can afford medical care to tend to your health. You can even afford the "luxury" medical services like massages.

As you can see, solving the financial problem will help reduce stress and therefore support overall good health and wellness. For those who say "The love of money is evil", I would agree, but money isn't evil; it's the *love* of it that is. Money is a tool that can be used to help solve the challenges that come up in life. Money can create a more powerful future for you and your family. What's wrong with that? NOTHING! But you must believe this if you want to use money the right way.

Tell Your Story to Build Trust with Them

I recently finished reading a very easy to read, short book called *The 60 Second Sales Hook*, which had a straightforward way of telling a story. Why is this important? People almost mind-meld with the storyteller who is telling the story.

Think about it. When you are watching a movie, you end up "becoming" the hero of the film. Notice that it doesn't even matter the gender the hero is, you still become that person or want to be that person to some degree!

The reason I recommend understanding how to craft YOUR story is that it will better connect you to the prospect. I'm sure you have heard that customers buy from people they know, like, and trust. According to *The 60 Second Sales Hook*, it turns out that the following happens when you tell a story.

✓ Prospects will "know" you because you reveal yourself in a relatable way

✓ They will "like" you because you will win respect with authenticity

✓ They will "trust" you because you share your struggles and secrets

The following are the four parts to a simple story:

1. Identity
2. Struggle
3. Discovery
4. Result

Let's get into each step with an example for each:

☐ **Identity**: This is a sentence that identifies who you are. *"Hi, I'm Ron, a network marketer."*

Your Identity: _____

☐ **Struggle**: This is a sentence or two that describes the specific problem or struggle you have.

"For years I joined MLMs but kept spending more money than I made. I had become pretty jaded toward them and wasn't interested in joining any more of them."

Your Struggle: _____

☐ **Discovery**: A sentence about the thing that provided the solution to your problem.

    Example: *"A person I respected who was doing well financially, suggested I join his MLM company to see if it would work for me."*

Your Discovery: _____

☐ **Result**: A sentence describing how life is different since discovering and implementing the solution.

    Example: *"I am so glad I decided to join his company. This is the first MLM I have joined where I have made more money than I've spent and now have a nice lifestyle.*

Your Result: _____

Of course, you can add more to each of the areas, but don't go overboard. The beauty of this simple approach is that if you practice it, you can deliver it in a minute and make an excellent connection. You can also talk about your product experiences and do simple personal testimonials with it. Just be careful who your target audience is because you could get into compliance issues if you did this as an online video talking about how "this magic product helped solve my [*fill in the ailment here*]." Just don't go there and you'll be safe.

Visit my bonus page for the link to get the book, worksheet, and script. Over the years, I have come across many different story scripts, but I like this one the best because it is straightforward enough to effectively teach to others.

Help Them Craft a Believable Plan

One thing you can do with business builder prospects is to help them come up with their own WHY by assisting them to do a little dreaming. As kids, we dreamed all the time of places we would go, places we would live, cars we would buy, people we would marry, and many other things. We did this because we didn't think they wouldn't come true. We had no real-life experiences to hold us back.

Unfortunately, most people stop dreaming by the time they hit thirty years old. Why? Because life happens (work, marriage, family, TV, Facebook, etc.), and they realize that they are "stuck" in a grind. They don't see a way to be able to come up with the money and time to experience or buy things they once dreamt of. So, they "settle for" the life they have and push down their dreams. This makes it hard to get them to open with their dreams and goals. They are so far from some of those dreams that they have no idea that any of it might be possible.

YOUR MISSION is to help them see a way to manifest those dreams.

For example, you could share a path to the following income levels with them to get them thinking (and more importantly, feeling) this could be a neat pathway to take in their life. Ask which income level they would like to achieve in the short-term and long-term. They can choose from this list:

☐ An extra $200/month to pay for dinners out, house cleaning, or new toys

- ☐ An extra $500/month to pay for daycare or a new car payment
- ☐ An extra $1000/month to pay for a mini getaway, rent, savings or account deposits
- ☐ An extra $2500/month to pay for a mortgage payment, a nice vacation, or hope to drop-kick a part-time job
- ☐ An extra $5000/month to quit your job or to take nice vacations
- ☐ An extra $10,000/month so both husband and wife can quit their jobs and save for a nice home
- ☐ An extra $25,000/month to buy a vacation home and put money away
- ☐ An extra $100,000/month to buy whatever you want! You'd be a millionaire every year!

Have them list out some things they would like to have or experience. If you tie this into your story from the previous section, you will be well on your way to helping them know, like, and trust you to be their guide to a better future for them and their family.

It's magic because you can find all you need about their WHY, pain points, and other things that will help you better connect with them.

CHAPTER 11

Secret #9: Follow-Up Can Be Easy

I f you have been around network marketing or any sales program, you will have heard the expression: "The fortune is in the follow-up." The reason is simple. If you don't follow-up with a prospect, you'll never make any money.

But people are busy, so timing is everything. Consider your own life. How many offers have you personally received to buy something that you ignored or said, "No thanks"? Then, later in life, maybe even the same week, you ran across the same person (or someone else selling the same thing) and bought it from them after thinking about it more.

The moral is to never give up the first time that prospects say, "No, thank you." In fact, many sales trainers say to not stop until you have had seven "no" responses. Personally, I don't usually go that high because I don't want to feel like a stalker, but I think you get the idea that you don't stop at just the first "no."

This chapter focuses on automating your follow-ups because there is already a lot of information available on the internet about how to do it manually. Besides, automated follow up, done properly, is much more of a secret.

They Are Interested. Woo-Hoo!

Think about all of the hard work you did by prospecting them. Maybe you wowed them with your incredible products or service. Perhaps you talked to them about the business opportunity.

Then, you hear, "This sounds interesting. Can you send me some information? Do you have a website?" or something like that. You woke them up to your products or opportunity, and then they want more information or maybe even to sign up! If you wait too long to reconnect with them, then they will ask their friends, and someone else who is more than willing than you to follow up and enroll them, will do so. In fact, you might even see them at the next convention, all excited that they are on the convention stage as a new leader — on someone else's team!

Don't let this happen! You committed to your prospect, and you get to do just that. But what do you do? There is a lot of training about how to follow up with prospects. Some are product-centered, and others are business-centered.

The approach you choose is up to you, but all them require you to reconnect in a consistent and organized way.

There are two ways to reconnect with your prospects. One uses manual methods of picking up the "500-pound phone," sending texts, using Facebook Messenger, or emails for follow-up. However, if you are like most new distributors, you might suffer from a little fear about what to do next or what messages to send them.

Or maybe you are not well organized and have lots of slips of paper or napkin pieces with names and numbers on them but don't remember where you met the prospects, what their challenges or health concerns are, or even who they are.

For you, I would recommend a semi-automated app on your phone or computer that captures their information, automatically sends them the information they requested, and even reminds you to do your follow-up call or email. The better apps will also ask for information to put your contacts into groups and will automatically send out follow-up emails and text messages based on the group or campaign you put them in.

Let's get into each of these types of follow-up methods.

Manual Follow-Up

The manual method of following up with prospects requires you to be disciplined and very organized. Otherwise, you will either forget to call them back or lose the lead altogether.

As we've discussed, prospects buy from people they know, like, and trust. Following up is all about relationship building and giving them what they asked for (or need).

I recommend using a printed form that helps you track the stages of each of your leads. You will always be able to review the details of each lead you are about to call. All excellent training courses will include a prospect-tracking worksheet you can use to stay on top of it. The better forms are highly optimized for your business and even tie into weekly tracking forms.

Knowing what their issues are will make you appear much more professional and interested in them, which will help with the essential elements of know, like, and trust.

Daily review of your "hot leads" will help you avoid forgetting to reconnect.

Automated Follow-Up

Contrary to all the artificial intelligence stuff you hear about on the news, computers are still good at one thing: repetitively doing mindless tasks. The challenge in the past was that it required being a software developer to figure out how to make computers do what you want. If you didn't have those skills, it would cost hundreds to tens of thousands of dollars to develop – way outside the reach of everyday small-business owners.

Mobile Apps Can Simplify Your Life

The great news is that in just the past few years, very powerful software has become available to you on your smartphone in the form of apps. You already use powerful apps like Facebook, Messenger, texting, email, Twitter, Instagram, and others to send and receive messages with friends and business associates. Here are a few more examples:

> ➢ Web browsers to access the internet (Chrome, Safari, Firefox, Internet Explorer, etc.)
> ➢ Video conference apps for live meetings with your teams
> ➢ Street and hiking map apps so you don't get lost

➢ Banking apps to manage your finances

➢ Password apps so you don't forget passwords

Apps can simplify your life in so many ways. They can also simplify your connection and follow-up process with prospects.

You can now download a simple-to-use app to completely automate the follow-up process you previously did manually on paper receipts and tracking systems. The crazy thing is these apps are not that expensive for what you get out of them. Let's face it; you probably spend more than five dollars on a fancy coffee and don't even really think twice about it. What if you skipped a few of those coffees in a month and put that money into an app that could save you tons of time and boost your business to new levels by allowing you to follow up in a more timely manner? You could be a couple of cups of coffee or a few bottles of water away from making follow-ups a breeze!

Do the Heavy Lifting With Your Smartphone

Here are some of the advantages of using automation for your follow-up:

✓ Reduced stress: Think about how much easier it will be and how much more time you will have in your life if you don't need to find those little pieces of paper you wrote prospects' names on!

✓ No more tracking sheets to keep all the prospects organized.

✓ Daily reminders of who to reconnect with and when.

✓ Very professional approach to connecting with new prospects.

✓ No more picking up the "500-pound phone" to call a person whose number you wrote down on a slip of paper, a
napkin, or store receipt.

✓ No crushes to your ego: If they don't reply, no worries;
your automation will keep following up for you. No more
sinking feeling of no one picking up the phone or respond-
ing to your text. When they do respond, it will feel good to
pick up the phone again!

A good app will help you with a daily task list and multiple
ways to follow up with prospects in the way they prefer (phone,
text, email, messenger, etc.).

Possible App Scenario

Here is an example of how you could easily add a new contact
using a simple app with hidden sophistication.

Imagine you meet Susie, and the conversation gets to your
amazing product and you "wow" her with it.

She says, "WOW, this is nice. Where did you buy it?"

You respond, "These are things I sell in my business, so you
can get them from me."

Susie says, "Do you have a business card or website?"

You say, "I don't have any cards with me, but I can do better."
Then you pop open your mobile app and say, "Susie, what's your
email address? I'll send you a link to an easy-to-understand website that will explain everything."

After entering it, you say, "Great. If you want, I can text the link to you right now. Would you like that?"

She says, "Yes," and you enter her cell number.

Next, you click on the desired "campaign" (automated follow-up email and text message sequence) you want to add her to, and you see a dropdown selection of things like these:

☐ Product prospect

☐ Business prospect

☐ Event gift

Alternately, you can just create your own selection and choose that one.

Want to add her as a friend on your phone too? (Maybe she's not just a business contact.) Just click the "add to phonebook" checkbox to do that.

Next, you click all the groups you want to add her to. Examples include:

☐ Met at the farmers market

☐ Hot lead

☐ Massage therapist

☐ Dentist

☐ Animal lover

☐ Mom

☐ Loves BOGOs

Of course, you can create your own groups if you prefer.

Next, you can add a follow-up reminder task in a day or two that will pop up on your mobile app.

You can also use the notes area to write in anything else that's important. Examples would be "Wants product info" or "Son has a knee injury" or "Gets frequent headaches," or something else that is important to her.

Seeing these notes will help you later when you get a follow-up reminder in your automated "Today's Tasks" list.

Then you click "Save" and their phone goes "ding," and Susie says, "WOW! That was fast!"

Now the heavy lifting begins! The automation takes over and sends you both personalized follow-up information emails.

The app[2] should be simple enough to not require you to use the website if you are happy with the default selections or until you want to start customizing them.

Recommended App Features and Functions

Here are some of my strong recommendations for the essential features and services you'll want to have in an excellent mobile follow-up app:

1. **Is simple to learn and intuitive to use.** If not, you won't use it (or at most, you'll use it for only a few months).

2. **Won't lose your data.** It would be very frustrating to store the data and then lose it. Ever tried adding a new prospect into your mobile phone book (yes, the one with 1000 contacts) and then forget the person's name so you don't know where to find it? You might as well have just lost the piece of paper! That's frustrating!

3. **Is highly automated.** It should be easy for you to use (with all the complicated stuff hidden away). You don't

---

[2] If you would like to get a free trial of our patent-pending app called *Simple Connector* CRM, visit *SimpleConnector*.com. It does all the above and more!

want to have to learn the intricacies of programming automated email sequences, websites, and task reminders.

4. **Offers a simple way to broadcast an email from the app to the chosen group(s) of people.** Perhaps you want to send today's BOGO to a select BOGO group. Or, maybe you want to send a group email to your team builders or hot leads or new distributor or customer, etc. You get the idea.

5. **Includes pre-canned automation sequences but also provides a way to customize both automated and broadcast messages.** Maybe the canned email and text message sequences are too long, or the messages don't feel personalized from you. You might want a custom email sequence you can drop people into when you enter their name or at some later time.

6. **Is highly optimized for your MLM business.** If it isn't, it probably won't be intuitive, easy to set up, or easy to use.

7. **Works offline.** Your app must be able to capture information when you are offline and automatically work correctly (like text messages) when you are back online. Examples include meeting someone on a hike, in a bad cell area, out of the country, on an airplane, or within an overloaded cellular network (think 30,000 people at the convention). You will expect your app to work in all conditions, automatically.

8. **Works across various message services.** It should allow you to call, text, message, and email messages when following up manually.

9. **Easily allows you to send prewritten broadcast messages to groups.** Having pre-written emails you can customize that can be sent to your custom groups of people from your smart phone will save you a lot of time.

10. **Easily set the next follow-up date.** If we don't stay on top of it, people you meet will fall through the cracks. The mobile app should have a simple way to add a follow up task for days or weeks into the future. Then, when the day arrives that the task is to be completed, it will pop up to remind you.

11. **Sends helpful email notifications for you.** The app should allow you to send automated reminders to yourself in any of the automated email campaigns, so you know what the prospects received. The emails could be the same or a shorter summary of the emails sent out.

12. **Sends helpful email reminders for you to do things.** For example, eleven days after Susie enrolls, it should remind you like this: "It has been almost two weeks since Susie joined your team. How is she doing?"

13. **Is low cost so your downline builders can also afford to use it.** A low cost allows them to duplicate what you do as they build their business.

14. **Includes a web "back office" for advanced users that allows all kinds of customization** The ability to customize automated campaigns, emails, and texts will enable advanced users to be able to stay on the same platform rather than having to learn a new one as their business grows.

15. **The web "back office" should include an option for users to easily create custom websites linked to their campaigns and have a way to buy custom domain names.** It should allow importing and exporting of contacts and data, and it should provide a calendar interface to help you see past and future tasks.

16. **Provides a way for creators of campaigns to share them with their team and maybe even sell them!** Once you create your cool campaigns, emails, and websites templates, you should be able to "duplicate" and share them with your team. You will save them time and will help them build faster.

17. **Provides a simple way to do the following:**

    ☐ List today's tasks with the ability to quickly move each to the future and connect in multiple ways (phone call, text, FB Messenger, email).

    ☐ List contacts with different sort options (date, when met, team, last seven days or other sorting tags).

    ☐ Add a new contact, select campaign, add notes, add new contact to multiple groups, and a personal referral, all from an easy-to-understand single screen.

    ☐ Send customizable prewritten broadcast announcement emails to chosen group(s).

Using automation can save you a lot of time when prospecting for your business. It can also help you significantly in the nurturing phase of a business, which occurs after a prospect has signed up and is now either a distributor or customer. Each type of recipient would benefit from a campaign personalized to their needs and wants, so be sure to group your contacts correctly. You wouldn't send automated emails about how to enroll people to someone who just wants to buy products!

The ability to send personalized email broadcasts from your phone to specific groups of people is also very useful. For example, you could send monthly specials to all who are in the "Wants BOGO info" group. In this case, these could include both customers and distributors.

Face it, automation is here to stay, and it is already making lives better for network marketers who are taking advantage of it. For those who don't, there are always forms and pencils, calendars, and of course, the 500-pound phone.

A patent pending app that meets the above goals is available. Use the link below to a special *Beyond the Products* book buyer signup offer.

https://SimpleConnector.com/btp-gift

CHAPTER 12

Secret #10:
Understand How You Can Get Paid

W hen I joined my network marketing company, the first thing I did was extensively study the compensation plan to see how I could make money. I figured that anyone starting a new business would do the same, but I was wrong!

In fact, there are many distributors who don't even know how they get paid! They receive a check in their mailbox or a deposit in their bank account, but they have no clue how to calculate how much they have earned.

Often this is because they came into the business for the products, found themselves talking about them, and started growing a business without realizing it. Others just get overwhelmed with all the complicated math, or they have been given a very watered-down version of how the compensation plan works from their upline. Whatever the case may be, understanding how it all works for you can be very motivating and empowering!

In this chapter, I will explain a little bit about compensation plans and more importantly, the different phases of business building and the associated way that you can earn higher bonuses.

By the way, if you don't care about the details, that's fine. At a minimum, spend enough time to understand your company's primary way to get paid with the phase I bonuses so you know where to focus your efforts. If you want to plan into the future, then it would be worth the time to understand the phase II and phase III bonuses.

Realize that most MLM company compensation plans are usually a hybrid of the various bonus types mentioned so money is available for new distributors, ones who have been in for a year or two, and those who are at top leadership positions. There must be something in it for all levels of distributors or there will be holes that slow or stop growth of the company.

 Finally, companies reserve the right to change the plans, at will, which could either help or hurt your income. Often, the compensation plans start out with the company's best guess of what will work to quickly build the company network and sales. But, because of "clever" distributors who find loopholes in the compensation plan or payment rules, companies change the rules so they don't lose too much money.

Make sure to have a current copy of the company policy manual to keep abreast of any changes. Your approach to building your business will need to factor in any changes of the compensation plan.

How Much Can You Earn?

Most companies publish an *Opportunity and Earnings Disclosure Summary* each year. (Search the internet for it if you can't find it in the documents supplied by your company or upline.)

Some are a few years behind, but they will show you the percentages and/or average monthly or annual earnings of each rank of the company. There are no promises you can earn these income levels, but at least you can get an idea of the approximate rank you should shoot for to achieve a targeted income level for your business.

That said, distributor income can range from just a few dollars a month, to millions of dollars a month, depending on the size and structure of your team and the company compensation plan. In 2020, the Network Marketing industry is valued at over 150 billion dollars. There is money to be made!

Compensation Plan Types

There are a variety of types of compensation plans that MLM companies have created to pay distributors. The names of the plans typically describe the required structure to receive the bonuses.

As a rule, about 50% of the sales of products is paid out in bonuses and commissions. The rest is captured for corporate infrastructure and profit.

Most of the newer company compensation plans are hybrids of one or more of the plans listed below. Note that this is not an exhaustive list but focuses on the more common ones in the industry. Your company will probably use one or more of the types of bonuses below. Review your policy manual for details about your specific company's compensation plan. Also, search online for more details of the plan types.

I will provide an overview of the following plan types:

➢ Stairstep Breakaway – Distributors break away from leaders when they achieve a specific rank

➢ Unilevel – Single level with unlimited frontline

➢ Binary – Two-legged structure that pays on the shorter leg

➢ Home Party – Home parties to share and sell products and recruit new distributors

➢ Generation – Distributors get paid on generations of distributors who have reached a leader rank/sales volume

➢ Matrix – Paid when required distributor levels and positions are filled

➢ Hybrid – Combination of plan types

Stairstep/Breakaway

This plan is one of the oldest plans in network marketing. When distributors increase their rank or volume to a certain point, they "break away" from the sponsoring distributor. The sponsor will then receive a smaller fixed percentage or override of the total volume of the distributor who broke away. Distributors continue to sponsor people on their front line. When a certain number of distributors have broken away, they achieve higher levels of leadership ranks and bonuses. Example companies that use this type of compensation plan include Amway and Arbonne.

Unilevel

Distributors sponsor new customers and distributors on their front line and receive a fixed percentage of the sponsored customer and distributor orders. Multiple levels exist and a percentage is paid out with each level. Sometimes the percentages increase and sometimes they decrease with each level. Some companies allow distributors to place new people at levels below their top level and earn a percentage of their orders. There is usually a cap to the number of levels that companies pay out bonuses. Example companies include Melaleuca and dōTERRA.

Binary

As the name implies, each distributor has two legs. Typically, the company pays out a bonus based on the shortest of the two legs. A few companies create a formula that includes both legs. Typically, one leg is built by people above you and the other is built by you, your sponsor, and your downline. I have seen earning caps on some of them, but some companies allow you to start over again in a new position. Example companies include Herbalife and Isagenix.

Home Party

This plan focuses on group events called home parties to recruit customers. Most of the time a host invites friends to their home and a distributor comes to do a show and tell presentation. The host then would receive free or reduced-price products if they are not already a distributor, otherwise, the new customers are placed on their front line. The distributor then gets paid immediately from the purchases at the party. This approach is more popular with women than men. Two examples of companies that use the home party approach include Pampered Chef and Tupperware.

Generation

Companies that implement generation plans pay out bonuses to people they sponsor until they reach the same leader rank. When that happens, they usually get a fixed percentage of all the people of the distributor who has reached that rank. As the sponsoring distributor continues to rank advance, they can then become eligible to multiple generations of distributors.

Matrix

Companies that use a Matrix plans pay bonuses to distributors who fill in all the positions of each level of a matrix. For example, a 3x3 matrix consists of 3 levels of 3 distributors or customers each. When the first level is filled up you receive a first level bonus. As each level is completed, you earn that level's bonus. The bonuses are usually considerably higher as the levels get deeper. BUT, if any position doesn't get filled, then no bonuses will be paid at that level or below. Any "holes" in the structure block bonuses to all levels beyond that level. (See the section on breakage, below.)

As an example, a 3x3 matrix would imply three distributors at the first level, each with three distributors of their own, who would each have three more distributors of their own again. The total number would be forty. The math goes like this: (1 + 3 +

(3x3) + (3x3x3) = 40), including your order. That's a lot of people. Three levels of three distributors sounds easier than forty distributors, doesn't it? If you want your matrix bonus, the end of the month can get crazy filling forty holes with orders!

Hybrid

Most new companies will include a combination of the above types of plans. For example, some companies are based on a Unilevel plan, but includes a matrix structural bonus along with other bonuses that kick in depending on the performance of the distributor.

Other companies pay out in a Unilevel plan but include a breakaway plan with distributors reach a certain leadership rank. Distributors above them can get paid generational bonuses on each of the legs that broke away.

Many times, compensation plans can be complex and take many hours or days to understand. Start by learning the bonuses that most directly applies to you where you currently are in your journey. There is no need to completely understand all the higher bonuses until you get to a point where it does matter directly to you. Otherwise you will waste valuable time. I've wasted lots of time doing this – just ask my upline.

Breakage & Compression

To prevent freeloaders from taking profits from distributors who are working hard, companies include either breakage or compression into their compensation plans.

Breakage is unearned and unpaid commissions and is usually returned to the company as increased profits. Compression occurs when distributors don't make the minimum qualification to earn commissions. Many companies require distributors to purchase a minimum number of products each month to qualify for their bonus payment. If they don't purchase the minimum, the commission they would have earned is taken away from them and either paid upline to the first distributor who qualifies for it or that commission goes back to the company either as more profit or the company uses it to pay some other bonuses to high performers.

As mentioned earlier, a distributor building a matrix with a missing order at level 1 would block all level 1, 2, and 3 bonuses from being paid. This lost money is kept by the company.

Three Business Building Phases

In general, bonus money comes from customers buying the company's products and is paid out to distributors depending on their sales, rank, and structure of their personal network.

Product flow creates the money for bonus payouts

Let's take a high-level look at the types of bonuses that get paid out to distributors and how they can be earned.

From my experience, I see three distributor business building phases:

> ➢ Phase I: Retail Selling (Sell products to customers for a profit)

> ➤ Phase II: Business building (Sponsor other distributors who sell products to customers for a profit)
> ➤ Phase III: Team Building (Build teams of leaders who recruit more leaders)

Each of these business phases requires a deeper level of commitment to building a business.

Phase I Bonuses

Phase I bonuses can be earned by any distributor who sells products by either selling them directly or by having customers visit their retail website and making purchases online.

Distributors don't need a serious commitment to build a phase I business. Buying some products at wholesale and selling products at retail to friends and other customers will get you Phase I bonuses. These types of bonuses typically will range between ten dollars to thousands of dollars a month depending on the company's compensation plan and the price of the products you sell.

I call this level or bonus phase, "hobby income." A distributor could quit at any time without any significant change in lifestyle.

Phase II Bonuses

Phase II bonuses are business builder bonuses. This phase can help a distributor earn a many thousand dollar per month income. These bonuses are earned when a distributor signs up other distributors who also want to sell products at retail.

Usually, this happens when someone you have signed up sees you making money and asks if they could do it too. They would like some income and therefore become distributors.

This income level could be enough to leave a lower-paying job or provide a nice way to cover a car payment, house payment, or even the cost of a vacation. Although higher income can be made at this level, it will generally be better to transition into the next phase if you want to make the big bucks MLMs can provide.

Phase III Bonuses

Phase III bonuses are for distributors who have committed themselves to become network team leaders in their MLM company. Phase III bonuses can reach into the millions of dollars a month for leaders with huge teams in some of the more established MLMs. Tens of thousands of dollars a month for newer MLMs is a very practical goal, though.

These bonuses are for people who have decided to put their business front and center of their financial future. As network leaders in their MLM company they can reap the rewards that come with that role. This phase requires not only time and energy to build your business, but always comes with some personal growth. For example, they discover success is about their team, not themselves.

To be a good leader, you get to become a good servant. You get to put your team's goals ahead of your own. You receive personal joy from their achievements and triumphs as they push past their limiting beliefs. Most of your time is spent mentoring, coaching, and inspiring your team to greatness rather than selling products.

For me, the greatest skill I have developed as a Diamond is infinite patience. This is an all-volunteer army so you can't manage your team. You get to lead them, which is a lot more fun for everyone.

Are You Spinning Plates?

If you are a distributor who is working to earn Phase III bonuses, it can feel like you are spinning plates at the end of each month. If this is the case, make sure you are leading others to build a team, rather than managing them to sell products. If you are managing them, spend the money and time to learn how to lead and inspire. Otherwise, you will have a stressful life and never really get your time back. You'll become a slave to your business, and it will own you, instead of you owning it. You might as well have a job. Check out secret #1, "Lead, Don't Manage," for more help in this area.

Companies Selling Like MLMs

If you just want to sell products for commissions and don't care about the networking aspects of MLM companies, there are a couple of types of MLM companies that could provide a higher income that can reach into the tens of thousands of dollars per month:

> ➢ Some companies are direct sales companies masquerading as MLMs which sell high-end products costing

hundreds to thousands of dollars and therefore don't really provide long-term residual income. (e.g. How many $150 water filters or $1500 water filtration systems do you sell per month... to the same customer?) This forces you to have to be constantly looking for new customers if you want to keep making money.

➤ Some companies sell programs, not just products (like weight-loss) that cost hundreds of dollars a month. Eventually, most of the high-end subscriptions end and the residual income from them lowers or disappears completely. (e.g. customers lose the weight and don't need as much of the product to maintain the weight loss.)

Both company types tend to require higher level skills in direct selling or weekly/monthly customer support. Both are really trading time for money in the long run. In the short run, though, each could provide much needed income via direct product sales.

Don't Lose Money When Selling Retail

If you are a distributor who buys products at wholesale and sell at retail, make sure you don't lose money. You may be buying the products at a 20% to 30% discount from the retail price but short-changing yourself when calculating the "retail" price you charge your customers. Also, don't forget to factor in your shipping and any taxes, if appropriate.

The math below will show you how to convert wholesale to retail. Don't simply multiply your retail discount percentage when converting it back to retail price.

Engineering geek/math warning: Skip below if you hate math. But, if you don't want to lose money selling stuff for a retail price that you buy at wholesale, then plod through the next section to determine your retail price markup multiplier.

Don't fall into the <u>false math</u> argument that if you save 25 percent as a distributor you would only add 25 percent (.25 times the cost of what you paid) to get the retail price.

In this example, the retail price you should sell at is calculated by multiplying your wholesale price by 1.33 rather than 1.25. If you make the mistake of selling it at 1.25 times the wholesale price, then you will lower your profits by 6 percent. For example, a product selling for $50 wholesale should be sold for 1.33 x $50 or $66.50. If you multiplied it by 1.25, you would sell it at $62.50 and lose $4.

The selling price would be your total cost (including shipping) divided by (100% minus your wholesale discount percent). This is what the equation looks like:

$$your\ selling\ price = \frac{your\ total\ purchase\ cost}{100\% - wholesale\ discount\ percent}$$

For example, if the total cost of the products you want to sell is purchased for $100 (with a 25% retail discount from your company), then you would calculate your retail selling price as follows:

$$your\ selling\ price = \frac{\$100}{100\% - 25\%}$$

But 25% = 0.25 (and 100% = 1) so completing it, you have:

$$your\ selling\ price = \frac{\$100}{1 - 0.25} = \frac{\$100}{0.75} = \$100\ x\ \frac{1}{0.75}$$

$$= \$100\ x\ 1.3333 = \$133.33$$

Or

$$your\ selling\ price = \$133.33$$
$$(Your\ markup\ multiplier\ \text{is}\ 1.3333)$$

So, your selling price would be $133.33 for your $100 purchase, not $125. You would have lost $8.33 if you sold it for $125!

Just plug in your normal retail to wholesale discount percentage into the above formula to get your "markup" price formula you will sell it to your customers. Again, don't forget to add your costs for shipping and sales tax, if appropriate.

Sorry for the math, but my engineering geek had to come out somewhere! Maybe you'll make a little more money now.

CHAPTER 13

Secret #11: Pick Your MLM Company Carefully!

Picking the right MLM company to join depends on many factors. In the end, it must feel right for you. If the company you are evaluating seems too good to be true or you see lots of gold watches and chains, fancy cars, and hard-core sales techniques, run, don't walk, in the opposite direction!

One thing to mention is that ALL of the factors in this chapter must be met, or passive income will not be there in the long run. So, pick your company, carefully!

I'm Too Late... You're Already In!

I suspect that most people reading this book probably are already in an MLM so this chapter might be a bit late. But, if you find yourself in a company that is not working out for you, read this chapter and see if any of the warning signs are there that could explain why it isn't working out. It is never too late to re-evaluate your decision until you are already making the big money. At that point, you have already proven it can work, so it doesn't matter.

If, however, the "rules have changed" for your company to the point where it is much harder for new people joining to be successful, then read this chapter because the writing may be on the wall that your own income may disappear.

MLMs depend on new distributors coming in and being successful or the entire "pyramid" collapses. Hundreds of MLMs disappear each year leaving high earners with zero monthly income overnight from them. This can be a real challenge if they have started to develop a higher lifestyle that depends on those checks coming in every month.

> *Golden Advice: As you reach higher bonus levels, take the money you earn from your MLM above what you need to survive and invest it into something else. Then, use the income earned from that investment to live on. That way, if your MLM disappears, you will not have to sell everything to survive because you are already living within your means.*

More MLM Company Evaluation Factors

In the last chapter, I discussed compensation plans and how you get paid, which is important. In this chapter, I'll discuss other factors which are also important to think about when evaluating MLM companies:

- ✓ Product Breadth and Demand
- ✓ Founder Experience and Agenda
- ✓ Training Tools and Systems
- ✓ Motivation of Upline Leaders
- ✓ Personal Fit to Company Culture

Product Breadth and Demand

This is a critical cornerstone of the long-term survivability of a network marketing company. If you want customers to keep coming back to you for more, then products must be:

- ☐ Uniquely available from your company
- ☐ Effective to solve a customer problem
- ☐ Priced fairly
- ☐ Have a no-hassle return policy

In addition, if distributors are required to buy them to earn bonuses, there must be a nice variety of products or they will start piling up in the garage, just so the distributor gets paid. One can only drink so much juice, eat so many vitamin pills, or use so much soap. You get the picture.

I am still finding soap in my bathroom cabinet from one MLM over 25 years ago. Great soap, but seriously, how much does a person need? 😊

The most important thing is that the customers must like your MLM company products enough to buy them regardless of the "MLM money-making" opportunity that encourages distributors to buy them to earn their bonuses.

Founder Experience and Agenda

The reason your MLM company exists should be clear from the founder's mission statement. Did they start the company to change the world... or add to their wallet?

MLMs come and go each year and many founders are serial MLM company starters. They really don't care about the products, tools, training, etc. Their focus is to make as much money as they can before the company goes out of business.

You'll recognize some of the signs like hiring famous sports figures or celebrities to push the products, wearing expensive watches, driving fancy cars, and doing massive presentations, like Hollywood events. Everyone jumps in for a chance to meet this cool person and gets sucked into the hype, not even caring what the products are. Flashing red lights for these MLMs! These companies would be lucky to last 5 years. Then the owners are off to start another one all over again after they have made their fast money.

On the other hand, if the founders of your company want to change the world and leave a legacy for their kids, not flashing Rolex watches, and driving fancy cars, but are normal "folks" then their company may have a chance. Why? Because they will do everything possible to make sure the company survives in spite of the inevitable ups and downs of the business. They are the ones who will go without pay if they must so that distributors receive their earned bonuses and promised products. They are not full-of-hype salespeople.

In other words, the founders are looking out for you, instead of themselves. Of course, they want to make money too. That's why they started a business rather than a charity. But you can tell they are heart-centered people who want YOU to be successful because they know that if you are successful, they will also be over time.

Training Tools and Systems

It is critical to include training tools and systems to help new distributors get started quickly. Without them, the excitement of a new distributor will wane as they become frustrated burning through all their friends. I'm sure you have heard the objections: (*also see Secret #7*)

> ➢ This is a pyramid scheme
> ➢ It's too expensive
> ➢ I don't have time
> ➢ "What did you get hooked into, *this time*?"

A good company (or at least top distributors) will provide tools like:

☐ A web-based back office to track your business

☐ Training videos and courses to teach the basics

☐ Large group events like conventions to excite and educate

☐ Special events for top performers to teach leadership

☐ Recognition events for top performers and leaders to motivate them (and their team)

☐ Social media tools to make it easier to "spread the word"

☐ App-based tools to make it easier to build their business when distributors are mobile (e.g. *SimpleConnector.com*)

Systems should also be in place to help distributors duplicate their upline. Duplication is the key element for a successful network marketing business. Without it, distributors will more than likely try their own approach without success, burn out, and disappear.

Motivation of Upline Leaders

The distributor who signs you up can greatly influence your business success. If you sign up with a distributor who signed up two days ago from one of their friends who signed up the same night as one of their other friends, chances are they won't know how to take you under their wing and guide you to your personal success.

On the other hand, if you sign up with an intergalactic diamond who is just cashing $25,000 monthly checks from a business they built 20 years ago, you might also struggle since they may not be very motivated to spend the time required to help you get started properly.

If you sign up with someone who is actively building their business and has achieved perhaps a lower leadership level, then you might be the perfect person to help them reach the next level they are looking to achieve. Expect lots of help from them to quickly build your business!

The team you enroll with can either help or hurt the speed of your business growth. Make sure to ask them questions about *their* goals. Find out if they are excited you joined their team and how they will help you build quickly. Ask them what tools and systems they duplicate as they build their business. Done properly, you will duplicate their success and you will all grow together, as a team, to the higher ranks and bonuses!

Personal Fit with Company Culture

Even if the products are great, the training is top notch, compensation plan has something for everyone, the founders are in it for the right reason, and your sponsor is amazing, if you don't resonate with the culture of the company, you'll lose steam.

For example, if you're a guy who is afraid to do presentations and your company plan does home parties selling cosmetics, it might not be the best fit. Maybe you are gal who is excited about clothing and the MLM is focused on financial services. Again, maybe not the best fit.

Not to say it is impossible, it is just harder. Remember that I'm the electrical engineer who was selling essential oils. Truly not my first calling, but I *had* to make money and I knew this was a path that could get me there. So, it IS possible. When you find something that rings true with all the above factors, you will probably have a winner for yourself.

All the Factors Mentioned Must Be Perfect!

As I mentioned at the start of this chapter, all the factors I discussed in this chapter must be checked off and perfect. This seems like a bold statement, so let me explain.

It's like a relationship with your significant partner. You have hard requirements that must be met, or the relationship will eventually end. Things like honesty, integrity, monogamy, etc. It is true that everyone has different requirements, but you have yours, and if they are violated, the relationship is doomed.

This is also true with MLM businesses. Here are each of the cases:

Example 1: Compensation Plan sucks

✖Compensation plan sucks

✓Product breadth and demand great

✓Founder experience and agenda great

✓Training tools and systems great

✓Motivation of upline leaders great

✓Personal fit to company culture great

All is great except the comp plan. There's no way to ever make the kind of money you want. Would you stay and work hard to build with this company?

Example 2: Product Breadth and Demand sucks

✓Compensation plan great

✖Product breadth and demand sucks

✓Founder experience and agenda great

✓Training tools and systems great

✓Motivation of upline leaders great

✓Personal Fit to company culture great

All is great except the products suck. Nobody would continue to buy the products. Would you stay there?

Example 3: Founder Experience and Agenda sucks

✓Compensation plan great

✓Product breadth and demand great

✖Founder experience and agenda sucks

✓Training tools and systems great

✓Motivation of upline leaders great

✓Personal fit to company culture great

All is great except the founders are serial MLM starters. They will probably close the company within 3 to 5 years. Would you stay there for long-term passive income?

Example 4: Training Tools and Systems sucks

✓Compensation plan great

✓Product breadth and demand great

✓Founder experience and agenda great

✘Training tools and systems sucks

✓Motivation of upline leaders great

✓Personal fit to company culture great

All is great except the training tools and systems suck. You never learn how to build the business and can't duplicate to your team. Would you stay there if you are working all the time and don't make much money?

Example 5: Upline leaders aren't there for you

✓Compensation plan great

✓Product breadth and demand great

✓Founder experience and agenda great

✓Training tools and systems great

✘Motivation of upline leaders sucks

✓Personal fit to company culture great

All is great except the upline leaders. They've made their money and don't have time to help you succeed or you are on one of their strong legs and they are focused on one of their weaker legs. You never learn how to build the business and can't duplicate to your team. Would you stay there if you don't make much money?

Example 6: Personal Fit to Company Culture sucks

✓Compensation plan great

✓Product breadth and demand great

✓Founder experience and agenda great

✓Training tools and systems great

✓Motivation of upline leaders great

✖Personal fit to company culture sucks

All is great except you don't fit in. You're a guy who is just not into home parties selling cosmetics and the company uses a home party plan bonus structure. How long would you stick around?

So, It Really Must Be Perfect!

See what I mean about everything having to be perfect. If any of them are missing, then the long-term "relationship" between you and the company will eventually end and your business will die.

CHAPTER 14

Secret #12:
What NOT to Do to Build Fast

This chapter contains a list of activities that are distractions and time wasters that don't directly lead to prospect enrollment and therefore business building.

I recommend you avoid if you want to quickly build your MLM business. I admit that I have fallen victim to many of them, and I lost a lot of time with minimal gain in every case. I genuinely hope you take this advice to heart because you will build faster if you avoid these common (and often tempting) pitfalls.

Some will seem counterintuitive, and you may even disagree with me on some of them, but if you are honest, you will realize I am right about them. We have enjoyed Diamond rank for many years, and I have witnessed or experienced how all these distractions slow people down toward their eventual goal.

Case in point*: I have been focusing on building my training courses and app, this book, and my SimpleConnector app over the past several years. This has caused our own business to slow down. I'm okay with this because one of my goals once I hit Diamond was to generate multiple streams of income and to create products to* *help distributors more effectively build their businesses. I chose to do that by creating digital and printed products. But this doesn't mean I've stopped building my MLM business. I use the same tools I am creating for you to support my business too, just at a lower level than a new builder.*

In any case, you get to decide what is important to you. You may want to push to top level leadership ranks. It is up to you once you get to Diamond, but by then you will have more free time and can make better business decisions without the time and money challenges.

Don't Focus on the Wrong Business Activities

It might seem obvious, but there is a big difference in the results of different business activities. Business **building** activities lead directly to enrolling prospects and include things like going out and meeting new prospects, taking them to classes, doing one-on-ones, and enrolling new team members. They will increase your business rank and your bottom-line profits. ALL other "business" activities are what I call business **support** activities.

I had an epiphany a few years back when I was creating my weekly planning worksheet for my online course: Business-building activities always involve prospects. If YOU are the only one doing the activity, then it is a **support** activity which adds NO additional direct money to your wallet. Support activities help *prepare* to build your business, at best, or distract you from building your business, at worst.

Business-building activities always involve prospects at some level. If YOU are the only one doing the activity, then it is a *support* activity, and it adds NO additional direct money to your wallet.

Don't Get Distracted by Other MLMs

There is an elephant in the room we should discuss: other MLM "opportunities."

You're a Target

As we grow bigger teams, we become targets of other MLMs. They see us as a fast track to building their business teams, so they want a "minute" of our time to prospect us for their new business. Typically, these predators hop from one opportunity to the next and are always looking for a bigger, better deal rather than just making the long-range decision to do the work required to build a stable business.

Some MLM predators will land in your downline to prey upon struggling distributors. Often, your downline who have been tempted by the other MLMs are looking for YOUR approval and hope you'll join them in the other MLM telling you how amazing you could be in their MLM with your "huge" downline. They somehow think it would be ethical for you to convince your team to move with you. This is ignorant thinking and always ends up badly for both of you.

Avoid "New and Shiny" MLMs

As someone famous once said, "Just say no." I'm not telling you to go through life with blinders on, but if you want to be successful with a PROVEN MLM, then don't get distracted with the latest shiny MLM. Remember that ground floor opportunities usually imply that people who come on later will be at a disadvantage. MLMs are all about duplication. If the new people can't duplicate the first ones, then the model fails. It becomes a crumbling pyramid.

New MLMs are being started every day by serial MLM CEOs, and most of them don't survive even five years. How would you feel if, in five years, your $20,000 checks stopped, in one month, forever? It happens all the time. One estimate is that there are about 3000 MLMs at any given time with 1000 disappearing and 1000 new ones each year. Think hard before joining another, especially if you are having success with your current one.

I don't know any successful MLM builder who has not been tempted by new and better-looking opportunities, and if we are honest, who hasn't joined other MLMs at some point? However, what looks better isn't always better in the long term. In these moments, take a step back and really look at the situation with logic and not with emotional excitement.

I'm Guilty of It Too

Just so you know I am human. I'm guilty of it too, and so have most of my leaders with various MLMs out there. It's just sooooo tempting. We try to justify taking it on by unrealistically thinking, *"How much time would it take, realistically?"* Then, after we have wasted our money and time, we hopefully come to our senses and realize we made a mistake and back out of it.

One fundamental truth is that you can't dedicate yourself and serve multiple masters in life, religion, or MLMs.

To truly build any successful business (including an MLM), you have to be wholly committed. You have to devote your life at least for a short time to build your foundation for the higher ranks. Putting your toes in the water won't work. You have to make the decision and jump in.

Read Your Company's Policy Manual

One thing to consider is that most MLMs have clauses in their agreements (you agreed to) that prohibit prospecting your team for other MLM business opportunities. It's one thing to sell products to them, it's another to prospect for business builders. Check the fine print of your MLM company. Some companies consider distributors "intellectual property" and can sue you if you prospect distributors in your downline or even crossline for another MLM company. Besides that, it's just not ethical. Realize that you are "stealing" the work of their upline and downline leaders if you pluck a distributor from one company for another.

Retention

The industry-standard measurement for retention is three months. If someone is still buying after three months, they are considered active. The retention value of most MLMs is very low, between 8 percent and 15 percent. Translation: Most customers quit after three months.

In contrast, the retention numbers for better MLMs are much higher, which means that enrolled people will remain active customers. This will help to generate that elusive passive income we all want.

So, if you are after long-term passive income, spend your valuable time building up your business in a single company that has proven itself. Choose wisely, because if you try to develop more than one MLM business, it will be very hard and maybe even impossible.

Don't Buy Business Cards

When you first start a new job, you usually get business cards, so it is only natural to want to get business cards as a new distributor, right? Wrong. They are a waste of money and time, and the reason is simple. When you are prospecting someone, you want the prospect's information so you can control what happens next. The best approach is not for you to give them your information and wait for them to call. They will usually say, "Great! I'll give you a call!" Then they'll walk away with your card, and the odds are very high they won't call. (How many people have you called back after they gave you their card?) You just lost control of the prospecting process.

Typically, if you ask them for *their* card or information *after you have given them yours*, they'll say, "Thanks. I have your information and I'll call you." Pushing to get their card or information at this point will start to feel creepy. In a dating situation, how would "Please go out with me!" feel to you if you had already told the other person, "Don't call me; I'll call you." If you don't have business cards, you can't fall into that trap. If they won't give you their information, would you really want to work with them?

So, how do you capture their information or share yours without the use of those little magic cards? Well, you can go old school and have a notebook with you and pray you can read their handwriting when you get home (or you own for that matter), or you can invest in a mobile-phone-based customer relationship manager (CRM) tool like *SimpleConnector* CRM mobile app. It creates an impressive, professional way to collect their information, and it gives them the information they requested as soon as you click the *save* button. When you hear that ding or buzz, you know that you are now connected and can keep the conversation going. That ding will lead to a customized website and, more importantly, to automated reminders for you plus follow-up emails and/or text messages for them.

Are you still tempted to get business cards? Think about how much time and money it takes to create and design a professional-looking business card. Not to mention that if you don't have them, you won't need to remember to carry them with you.

These days, we always have our phone. You will always have a way to capture their information and, even better, you can rest assured you will *automatically and instantly* follow up with them if you use a mobile phone app.

Don't Create a Custom Website

Ever feel like you need to have a custom website to build your business? If you've been following the logic of the discussion about skipping business cards, you will quickly realize that it is almost the same situation with a website, except that it takes weeks, not hours, to create a professional-looking website.

Another reason to skip this step is that if you give them your website, you just lost the upper hand once again. When the prospect says, "Do you have a website?" and you provide it, you once again lose control of the connection.

One Exception

The only exception I have for this is a simple website that is automatically generated and tied to an email automation app such as *SimpleConnector,* which sends them info as soon as they enter their contact information onto the form. Since it only takes ten to twenty minutes to personalize the website and link it to your automated email sequence, I'm okay with it. If you have the "gotta have a website itch," this is a simple solution that doesn't take a lot of time. Just make sure to leverage online-MLM-expert developed templates for websites, emails, and campaigns.

Also, have the prospect visit the site as soon as you meet them so they can fill out the "opt-in" form and get added to your contacts and start receiving the automated emails and text messages.

Don't Use Complicated Automation Software

NERD ALERT! This section gets into technical stuff that will probably not interest most distributors. Network marketers who want to know more about automated email systems might want to read this section. Read on if you are curious, but don't worry about missing out if you skip this section.

This is a topic that is close to my heart since I really enjoy automation systems. Getting a computer to do repetitive stuff that I don't enjoy doing is something I've accomplished in various ways and multiple jobs for much of my adult life.

I have tried many different email automation platforms, from *Aweber* to *Constant Contact* to *Infusionsoft* to *ActiveCampaign*. I even became a partner in promoting their systems. All are just too complicated to both learn and teach to others who are not technically oriented.

And if all the above isn't enough, I realized I could never duplicate the approach because of the high monthly cost. How many distributors would be willing to spend $50/month, let alone $350/month for the higher-end products?

Why I Created *Simple Connector*

I built *Simple Connector* to be easy to learn and use, duplicable, and low cost – perfect for my team and others to use to build their network marketing business.

It factors in all the things people need for belly-to-belly and now online prospecting and leaves the complexity hidden. It is intuitive to use, and it is super-low cost. It is the most economical app on the market for distributors, and I did this for a reason.

It isn't all about money for me. I want to see you succeed. You might recall that my life purpose is to help people become the best versions of themselves.

If new distributors can't afford a chosen automation platform, they won't buy it. If they don't buy it, they can't duplicate what you are doing to be successful. Everyone loses!

That's why *SimpleConnector* is simple to use with all the power you need of the more expensive platforms at a small fraction of the cost. It also has the option of a web backend for power users and leaders who want to be able to customize their websites, campaigns, groups, and emails. In fact, there is also a way to share campaigns, emails, and websites with your team to duplicate yourself even better! Ahhhh.

Out of the box, it will capture information, send texts and individual emails, and give you the ability to see today's tasks, to see a list (and optionally details) of all your prospects and contacts, and even to send emails to any group(s) you have set up, all from your Apple or Android phone.

Don't Ever Buy Leads

Ever put your name in a jar for some freebie at a restaurant or health fare? Guess where those names go many times? If you are lucky, you become somebody's lead for a cold call. If you are unlucky, they added your name to a generic "business builder lead list" sold to lots of entrepreneurs like yourself who are looking for easy leads they can prospect for their MLM business.

Lead buying is a perfect example of trying to take a shortcut. It sounds so simple. You think you are buying affordable leads of people who are looking for your business opportunity. You think that all you will need to do is call them up and send them to your website, and then enrolling as your newest business builder.

Uh-huh, get real. Every single lead is a cold call. You will need a script to read, and if you are lucky, you *might* have time before being hung up on to find out if the prospect is looking for a business opportunity. Of course, that is if they even choose to pick up the phone.

Do you listen to every cold call you receive during dinner or as you wake up? Or do you hang up? Why would you expect your cold call go any differently?

One of my downline distributors recently bought 150 leads, and not a single person signed up as a business builder in her business.

She spent MANY hours calling them, leaving them messages, and following up. Each session of cold calling took a couple of hours out of her busy life, and she had a professionally written script. She judiciously called ten leads a day, but after two weeks, and a few conversations with me, she realized this is not the way to build a successful network marketing business quickly.

Why? It's back to this essential question: "Whose needs are you filling? Theirs, or yours?

Everyone finds prospecting for leads to be a challenge. There is no shortcut to acquiring leads. Just learn how to do it the right way, and then start doing it. (Sorry to be so blunt, but tough love is sometimes required!)

Don't Take More Than One Course at a Time

This one is probably obvious to most people, but there are so many options these days for training to build your business, I had to bring it up.

There are many training systems out there for network marketers. The goal of most is to help you sell more products in some way or another or to hard sell to find business builders. Some are sales courses that push making the sale at all costs, even if it is just a single product purchase. Some are more healer-oriented and are developed to help you "share the products." Others are Facebook groups to help you understand more about the products. Some are well-organized training systems, but most are not.

Now that you have read my book, you know my focus is showing you how to find builders so you can create the long-term passive income you want. You know that I don't focus on selling the products. Instead, I leverage them to start the conversation that leads to the dream-building discussions so you can more quickly find potential business builders with a reason to transition to a better life.

My main point is for you to know that there are many competing training systems out there with different philosophies of how to be successful.

My warning is to avoid taking multiple courses at the same time. This can lead to confusion as to which approach to follow. When potential students come to me wanting to join my program, I ask them if they are currently in another course.

If they are already in a program, then I tell them to finish their course. I invite them to let me know later if they are still interested, so they can join at that time. The old adage that "You can't serve multiple masters" is true here too.

Just pick one, get through it, and then see how well it works for you. If not, then try the next one until you find one with an approach that resonates with you.

Stop Volunteering for Everything

When I joined my MLM company, I was the president of our homeowner's association, vice president of our swing dance club, and the secretary of an inventors' club. I also helped many people, for free, to determine if an invention they were considering was technically feasible. I was swamped and tired of being very broke!

I had forgotten the rule that TIME is your most valuable asset. And I was giving it all away for other people's benefit. People loved me for it, but I was still broke.

I also was part of a coaching program, and my coach told me something painful but essential that struck a chord with me. He said I was brilliant when I focused on one thing but broke when I didn't.

I gave myself this challenge: "How do I extricate myself from the process of giving away my time for free?" There were so many commitments I had made to so many people.

In my head, I knew if I wanted my life to change, I had to change something. So, I decided to stop volunteering for a while and pick one project to generate income. I knew this would change our family's future.

Remember, at that point I owed $100,000 in credit card debt and was maxed out on all my cards. Most of the debt was from investing in many of the internet marketing educations programs to make money on the internet. (Later, I discovered that most of the people who make money on the internet are the ones teaching how to do it. Go figure!)

So, I chose to focus and work hard for a few years to build our MLM business. As a result, I was able to get out of debt and develop new streams of income. Can this happen for you too? Sure, but you have to stop giving your time away for free. There are no shortcuts or promises, as I've mentioned throughout this book.

If you want to change your income level and are actively volunteering your time to help other people or organizations succeed, then you need to take a hard look to see if your financial situation can support this. Does it make LOGICAL sense to give away that much time to others?

I remember a saying that went like this: "You can only give from baskets that have something in them." Maybe it is time to stop giving so much away and start refilling the basket. Most of the "busy" people I meet are giving too much of their time to others. How about you?

My short message is simple: STOP IT! Watch this fun but thought-provoking YouTube video:

https://youtu.be/Ow0lr63y4Mw

Work on chopping down your commitments so you can recover some time to build your business. Also, consider using your kids as the excuse TO build your business, rather than an excuse not to do so. Working hard for a year or two to create a business that gives you your time back can be much more rewarding than waiting. Remember that your kids are watching you. So, teach them the right way to prioritize things to manifest the results you are seeking. Explain to them what you are doing. They won't be thrilled at first, so make the time you spend with them exceptional. Then build your business with the recovered time. Trust me. It's worth it. Ask any Diamond or above who has kids.

Don't Become a Product Expert

As I mentioned earlier, when I started my network marketing business, I did not think I had a chance of being successful because not only did I not know anything about our products, but I didn't even believe in them at the time. (Remember, most engineers don't do woo-woo.)

However, my lack of knowledge and belief turned out to be positive. Sound odd to you? Then let me explain why you should not become a product expert. I know this will be hard for some of you (especially medical professionals), but you have to realize that in order to build a successful MLM that creates passive income and gives you back your time, you have to do things that are clearly easy to duplicate.

The reason is simple. If the prospect says, "WOW, you're a natural at this. I could never learn that stuff or do what you do," then you've already lost. It might make your ego feel great, but it won't build your business as quickly as showing others how to find the answers to their own questions so they know they can do it too.

> *If you are the hero, then they will always come to you to be saved! If you want them to become the hero, then they have to believe they could do this too.*

If they feel they can be better than you, that's great; then they will have the belief right from the start that they can do it because you empowered them.

When people ask me what product to use if their nose is stuffy, I don't just say, "Use the respiratory product." I say, "I think that the respiratory product might work, but let's check the book, app, or online to see what is recommended. " After a few of these questions and answers, they want the book, so they don't need to ask me anymore.

The goal is to empower your leaders and customers to be their own product experts. Ultimately, this leads to more passive income for you because you won't need to spend as much time with them talking about the products. You can use the time to talk about helping them build their business, instead.

Plus, they won't call or text you at 2:00 A.M. with a sick kid so they can ask you what product to use!

Finally, if you need anything else to convince you, the FDA prohibits you from prescribing products for medically diagnosed diseases and illnesses. Doing so will eventually get you (and your MLM company) in trouble. So, why start down that path? Make sense?

If you are currently the product expert on your team, start weaning people off by showing them the books and apps. You could even hold some training sessions on Zoom or in person to showing them how to find answers independently.

Stop Consuming Online Social Media Content

Many people I know spend countless hours going down the rabbit hole of Facebook or other social media platform. They are *consuming* the content.

Funny thing is they tell me it helps them build their business. The truth is that if they spent the equivalent time prospecting people, in person, their business would grow a lot faster.

Even Rachel Hollis, a trendy social media expert, told distributors at a recent leadership event, "I don't consume Facebook content." Why? Because of the rabbit holes. It is pretty much a waste of time on many levels, but especially for your business. It will not help your business to find out that Susie's sister-in-law's niece just had her first poop — with photos to prove it. Sorry for the graphic visual, but I think you know what I mean.

The same thing applies to Instagram, Twitter, Pinterest, etc. They all are time sucks UNLESS you are posting content that attracts BUSINESS BUILDERS and not product buyers.

Nowadays, advertising on social media is even more critical because of all the privacy issues and because Facebook and the other platforms are making it much more difficult for you to get your message out to people organically. They want you to pay for advertising, which can be awfully expensive and require expert help if you want to reach the people you used to be able to reach for free.

Also note that if you try to run Facebook Ads, it will consume tens to hundreds of hours to figure it all out. And then, once you figure it out, they'll change it again.

Don't just believe me; ask anyone who does Facebook advertising. It's for the pros these days, not for the amateurs.

Don't Quit Your Job Too Quickly

This one should be obvious, but I continue to find distributors quitting their nine-to-five jobs too early. They start having some success with their MLM business, so they figure they'll be able to make more money faster than what usually happens.

They might be making $1000/month and they're not happy with their boss or commute or job. So, they quit their job to build their MLM business. Then, a peculiar thing happens. All the things that didn't get done because they were too busy in their job suddenly pop into view. WOW! They can "finally" take care of those things that weren't getting done.

Then, they end up NOT building their MLM business with that "free" time. Soon, they become financially strapped because they needed the job's $1500/month to cover all their current expenses, but the money isn't there. Then they panic that they quit too soon, so they try to find some temp work to cover the difference but end up not being happy with that situation either.

Now, they're trapped. They were initially on a practical path that would have paid off, but they got impatient. With just a little more patience, they could have developed enough MLM income to cover the lost job income, survived and even thrived.

Moving from a job to entrepreneurship is a challenge for most people. The reason for this is that jobs pay you for the activities you do, and entrepreneurs make money by the results they create.

To get paid from a job, you need to do three things:

1. Show up, when you're supposed to
2. Don't make waves (get along with people, and your boss)
3. Sometimes do your job

If you do that, you'll get a regular check. On the other hand, to get paid as an entrepreneur, you have to do ONE THING well:

1. Create enough value for your potential customers that they pay you for it

There is no mention of time, is there? That's because it could take you one hour or one week to create the value depending on your level of expertise or experience. The better you are at creating value, the less time you must spend doing it.

These subtle differences can mess people up when they are moving toward entrepreneurship. Master them, and you'll be massively successful. Don't master them, and you'll be back at your job sooner or later.

So, the moral of the story is to not quit your job too early. Make sure your network marketing income is where it needs to be to cover your job's current income and make sure to counsel upline for guidance. It is in everyone's best interest to do it the right way with the right timing, even if you just dying to leave that job!

Avoid Online Prospecting[3]

Do you feel it? Do you hear it? It's that sucking sound of the internet calling you. Everyone wants the holy grail of online prospecting for their business. They think, *"There are so many people out there. It has to be easy!"*

The truth is that online prospecting costs a LOT of money and takes a LOT of time and expertise to turn into a real business.

If you want to build quickly, you would be much better off meeting people in your hometown than starting an online business.

One exception to this is if you ALREADY have a large group of people who actively follow you. I'm talking about thousands of people who *already* read your posts, watch your videos, and attend your webinars.

Here's another problem, though: it is not easily duplicable! Do the people you find in your group also have thousands of people following *them?* If not, you will have to teach them how to do something you don't for them to build their businesses. What will that be? It will be the "Do as I say, not as I do" approach to business building.

In general, all the online marketers I know will agree with me (if they are honest). It is much harder to build an online business

---

[3] The only exception to this is if you use a tool like *Simple Connector* AND you use templates for the websites, emails, text messages, and automation campaigns that have been developed by online MLM masters.

than it looks. You will spend many, many more hours and spend many more dollars doing marketing online rather than doing belly-to-belly marketing offline.

Don't Exhibit at Farmer's Markets and Other Events

I know I will get some resistance from die-hard distributors about this but hear me out.

One of my leaders regularly has a booth at multiple farmer's markets in the area. She spends countless hours preparing product samples to solve multiple pet-related health and wellness-related issues.

Her events look like this:

- ☐ Spends hours preparing the product samples and smaller size product packages
- ☐ Loads up her car the night before the event
- ☐ Drives to the farmer's market early in the morning
- ☐ Sets up her booth and cover (it gets hot in the summer)
- ☐ Stands on her feet for eight hours the first day sharing her products to people passing by
- ☐ Enters them into contests ("to win a prize, just fill out this survey and put it in the bowl")
- ☐ Packs up her booth in her car at the end of the day
- ☐ Drives back home
- ☐ Takes her pets out for a walk
- ☐ Cleans herself up
- ☐ Crashes in bed!
- ☐ Repeats everything above for the second day

- ☐ Unloads her car
- ☐ Cleans herself up
- ☐ Crashes in bed!
- ☐ Starts the almost-cold-calling process the next day to follow up with all her leads

When I asked her how many **business builders** she has received from all the events she has done for the past eight years, she said, "**none.**" She says she uses the leads to plug holes for her MLM matrix structure to earn a higher bonus and she is a lower-ranking leader in our MLM!

Recently, I asked her if she wanted anything to change. She said she wants to go Diamond. What does she need for Diamond? Business builders. So, she stopped the farmer's markets to focus on finding builders and getting to Diamond.

My experience is that you meet lots of friendly people at the events, but they want the free samples and lower-priced products. They're not asking for a business opportunity. If you use farmer's markets and street fairs during the simmer (oops, summer) months, tell me this: how many real business builders have you enrolled? Be honest. Was it worth the countless hours and dollars you spent on the booths, supplies, resale tax licenses, and even wear and tear on your body? What has *your* experience been?

Imagine if you were to go downtown and walk into stores at 2 P.M. and starting a conversation with business owners about what is important to them in the same amount of time you spent at that farmer's market or street fair. Do you think you could find more business builders than at the farmer's market or street fair?

Conclusion

All the distractions in this chapter will either slow down or interfere with your progress towards a network of dedicated business builders. I know that some of this chapter's "not-to-do's" are openly promoted as "to-do's" by leaders, but if you ask them where they get their leads, they'll probably tell you it is through one-on-one connections with people they meet just doing their daily activities. Trust me, there are gazillions of people who want what you have. They just don't know it yet. So, go out and find them. They're waiting for you!

CHAPTER 15

BONUS:
Building Your MLM Business During COVID

The pandemic has certainly changed the way we build a traditional Network Marketing Business. It's pretty hard to have "product parties" when nobody can attend in person. There is nothing like being able to pass around products and hear the Ooooh's and Ahhhh's as participants experience them.

Then there is the difficult situation of the 6' rule when out and about prospecting for new peeps: "Here, catch this product and try it! Isn't it amazing?" Yeah, right!

Traditional MLM Prospecting is Dead Right Now

I have always preferred belly-to-belly prospecting to build my network marketing business, but the truth is it isn't very practical right now.

It's true that people who have established a nice large team have actually seen an increase in their team volume (thanks to wellness products and the like) but for those people who are just starting out, it has become a bit harder to "duplicate" their up-line's success using the traditional methods they teach.

Time to Re-Think Websites

In the previous chapter, I discussed things you should NOT do to build quickly. One of the things is "Don't create a fancy website" because it can take so much time and money to create the perfect site that represents you.

I don't know about you, but online business building is starting to look more attractive right now. Some obvious advantages include:

➢ Staying home keeps you COVID safe

➢ Takes less time if you automate properly

➢ Costs less than sampling products to prospects if you use the right tools like *Simple Connector*

➢ Is very duplicable if you do not focus on Facebook

➢ Can be very non-pushy if you learn how to prospect based on the buyer's journey (See my blog posts)

➢ Can be integrated with belly-to-belly prospecting when they finally let us back outside!

Of course, with the good, there are disadvantages too:

➢ Fewer spontaneous face-to-face meetings of new people

➢ Missing social interaction of in-person group classes

➢ You're going to have to learn something new — brain cobwebs and smoke coming out of your ear's kinds of stuff!

➢ Spending money on things you don't already spend money on (But you can keep the costs WAY down with the proper tools)

Add Online Prospecting to Your Business

So, here goes... I am now recommending that you start to supplement your face-to-face MLM business building with an online component.

Normally, I would say you should just dip your toes into it and start slowly. But the truth is COVID has changed all of that. If you just wait for things to get back to the way things were and shift too slowly, you will definitely fall behind the pack of those who are learning new stuff every day – even at this moment.

It's YOUR business and if you want to build it, don't be a victim of COVID. Bite the bullet and start learning how to go online.

There are online teachers selling "how to build your business online courses" that can cost $500, $1000, or more with private coaching. But WHO has that kind of money when they are starting out?

The truth is that I have spent the past 15 years learning how to build online businesses. I have spent well over $100,000 learning how to do it — probably double that! And I do not want you to make the same mistakes I made. There are low-cost ways to do it, but most were technically difficult to master.

Don't Be One of "THOSE" People

You do not want to be one of those distributors who are constantly pushing products on their Facebook friends and family, do you? Besides, when you depend on a company like Facebook for your business, you are taking a HUGE risk that they could change their algorithm (as they do constantly) or even shut down your account, with NO RECOURSE! — Yes, they do that too. The good news is that the light at the end of the tunnel is beautiful sunshine if you build online the right way... but could be a train if you don't, so make sure to choose wisely!

Going Online Using Traditional Methods

So, how do you go online? The traditional methods include:
- ☐ Websites (WordPress, Weebly, corporate MLM sites)
- ☐ Email (Gmail, Outlook, Hotmail, AOL)
- ☐ Facebook (both organic and paid advertising)
- ☐ Google (both organic and paid advertising)
- ☐ Pinterest
- ☐ Instagram
- ☐ Autoresponders (to send out emails and/or texts)
- ☐ Chat bots pretending to be human that answer questions
- ☐ Zoom (meetings and group classes)
- ☐ Online training courses
- ☐ Webinars (group classes)

I could go on and on but I'm sure you recognize some of the above. The traditional learning curve is steep! But I would never make you learn all that stuff! Lucky for you, I love to help make complex stuff simple for people.

The reason I created *Simple Connector* in the first place was to help belly-to-belly MLM prospectors automatically follow up with their prospects and team members. (Secret #9). But the primary customer for that product was traditional belly-to-belly MLM prospecting, follow-up, and team nurturing.

Going Online the Easy, Low Cost Way

So, I sharpened the pencil and burned some midnight oil and we added easy-to-learn and modify, websites to the platform and made it accessible online via your desktop browser.

We also added the ability to easily clone websites, emails, and automation sequences so you can share them with your team and others! You can even modify the imported stuff and then export them to your team to use.

Why is this important? Because the secret to going online QUICKLY is to duplicate MLM experts who create websites, emails, and email automation campaigns that would appeal to MLM prospects in the online world.

Sure, you could re-invent the wheel, but how much time do you have in your day? I don't know about you, but one thing I learned long ago is to do your "WOW" well and then pay others to do their "WOW"s. Besides, why would you want to learn and do stuff you could give to someone else to do?

I have a sign on my computer monitor. It says:

1. Eliminate
2. Delegate
3. Automate

First, remove things from your life that really don't have to be done. Next, give things that you don't like to do to others. Finally, automate the left-over tasks. Why? To give you the time to do the things you really want to do.

Simple Connector was created for me, my team, and now you, if you are interested. It will help you eliminate, delegate, and automate the things you really don't want to do to build your MLM business. I wish it had existed when I started my MLM business. I could have saved countless hours!

By the way, it is easy to learn and use and incredibly low cost!

No More Horse Driven Buggies

As I said in the beginning of this chapter, times are different today and they may never go back to "normal". You don't see a lot of horse driven buggies running around the dirt roads these days, do you?

That's because the horseless buggy (automobile) killed that market in a very short time. You are in the middle of times of change. You can either embrace it or hide in the corner hoping the old ways will come back. In the meantime, your "competition" will be learning how to add new ways to build their business... and taking away your prospects and even team members as they build.

If you are interested, you can learn more about this in my *Simple Connector* blog. I have lots of information there about online ways to build your MLM business. You can also get on my email list and receive lots of free training. I would love to see you one day on one of my zoom calls! And when it is safe to meet in public, I'd love to connect with you at a future *Simple Connector* event!

https://simpleconnector.com/blog

Check out one of my blog posts that shows how you can go ONLINE with your MLM business:

https://bit.ly/2ZUV45v

You can also download a mind map with 6 pages of details of how to go online by visiting the link below:

https://bit.ly/33nhZbq

Stay Happy and Enjoy the Journey

D o you get frustrated that things are not moving along as fast as you want? Did you want to get to a certain income level before a deadline but are frustrated you didn't make it?

I know builders who curl up like a ball in bed, depressed for days because they didn't reach the rank they wanted "in time."

Watch this bonus video lesson, "How to Stay Happy and Enjoy the Journey" and switch to a positive mindset. It's one of my training program students' favorite lessons.

I learned this lesson inside of an $8000/year coaching program – I'm saving you some big money!

www.BeyondTheProducts.com/bonuses

CHAPTER 17

Free Bonuses

W ho doesn't like free stuff? I know I do, so I have included some excellent free bonuses with this book. Included are:

➢ Free video: How to stay happy through the journey

➢ A free audio version of this book -- as soon as I record it

➢ A free trial of the *SimpleConnector* CRM smartphone app to help you build your business

You can access them by clicking the QR code links in each of the sections below. Enjoy!

www.BeyondTheProducts.com/bonuses

Free Audio Version of This Book

I enjoy listening to audiobooks. It saves me so much time because I'm not a speed reader. So, whenever I can, I check to see if the book I want is on Audible and buy it if it is.

A year ago, I tried something I have never done before (probably because I'm too cheap to buy both the printed and audio versions of books). I listened to the audio version at 2X speed WHILE reading the printed version of a book I had purchased from one of my coaches. My coach included the audio version with the printed version of the book. Since I had both versions, I figured, why not try listening while I was reading? Amazingly, my comprehension of the book was off-the-charts high!

I also noticed that sometimes the audio and words I was reading would fall out of sync. So, I would rewind the audio and re-synchronize them. At that moment, I realized that my concentration had drifted, but I would never have been aware of it if I hadn't been receiving the information from both my eyes and ears. Amazing. And powerful!

So, my gift to you is a free audio version so you can get to do the same thing if you want. Everyone who buys my printed book also receives the audio version for free. You'll be able to access the audio via the bonus page. I may also create an audible book for Amazon. Stay tuned!

Free Trial of the *SimpleConnector*™ CRM App

One of the most powerful ways to follow up with prospects and stay in touch with new friends and team members is by using automation to help you. So, I have also included a free trial of the patent pending *SimpleConnector*™ mobile phone app. You can use this app for belly-to-belly prospecting as well as internet-based lead capture and follow up.

SimpleConnector gives you a simple, intuitive way to connect you with prospects, friends, and team members right when you meet them. If you sign up before the price increases, you will be grandfathered in at the very low pricing.

Find out more by clicking the QR code below using the camera of your iPhone, a QR app on your Android, or visiting the *SimpleConnector* website with a special bonus for book readers.

https://SimpleConnector.com/btp-gift

Epilogue

Whew! That was a lot of information to absorb. That's why this book is organized as a reference guide rather than a "user manual."

If you take the time to learn and apply even *some* of the information in this book to your business, you should see some major changes, like leaders appearing where buyers once stood and more money flowing into your pocket because you FINALLY understand how you get paid.

If you received value from this book, then please pick up a copy for team members who could use some clarity about how to harness the amazing business opportunity in their hands.

My life purpose is to help others be the best they can be through my example. There may be people who think I'm doing it all wrong, but I am here to say that my life is not what it was a decade ago as I was sitting in my office wondering how I was going to dig out of $100K of debt. Network marketing works – IF you work it in a smart way – plain and simple!

Here's the big takeaway from this book. If you learn how this business works and then dedicate yourself to it for a few years, it can completely change your life in ways you can't even imagine today. It can work for anybody who wants it badly enough and is willing to learn new things, push past their limiting beliefs and act towards their goals.

Of course, no two people will build the business the same way. That's because no two people are the same. Some are on a fast track; others are slow and steady. Some focus on the products and others on the people.

I chose to develop a hybrid approach that leverages the products to start a conversation with my prospects and then shift the conversation to what they really want in life. Then, if they want to know more, I help them develop a plan to get what they are looking for and let them know I'm with them 100 percent of the way. That was true when I started, and it is still true today.

I am grateful to the founders of my chosen MLM who created an amazing company, my leaders for believing in me even before I did, and my tribe for trusting me to guide them on their journeys. Their amazing growth, both personally and financially, has helped us create our life as it is today.

I have no idea what tomorrow holds, but I know that network marketing will be a big part of it for as long as I am alive.

If you have thoughts of how I can improve this book or suggestions for additional content to include, please visit my contact page. (See QR code below) I'll read every one of them and respond to as many as possible.

Keep smiling,

SimpleConnector.com/contact

Glossary

1 on 1 – Personal meeting exclusively with a potential business prospect (or prospect and spouse) for the sole purpose of presenting the business opportunity to them.

Account Manager – A corporate employee assigned to assist a distributor who has achieved a leadership rank in that MLM.

Active – A distributor or customer who has purchased products within 3 months to a year. (Depends on the MLM)

Activities – Specific deeds performed to grow your business.

Audible – A division of Amazon dealing exclusively in audio works, especially audio books.

Back office – Your portal into the company website showing your product orders, commissions, and downline information.

Belly-to-belly – Another way of saying "face-to-face".

BOGOs –Acronym for "Buy One, Get One" free. BOGO specials are offered periodically by some MLMS to temporarily boost sales.

Builders – Distributors who want to build their own business by promoting and selling MLM products or the business opportunity to others.

Business Building Activities – Activities designed to bring prospects onto your business team. Examples include prospecting, follow-up, classes, etc. (as opposed to support activities)

Business Builder – See "Builder".

Coach – An individual who focuses on developing a certain skill set in another individual(s). Coaching holds builders accountable at their request.

CRM – Abbreviation for Customer Relationship Management software used to help with follow-up of contacts.

Crossline – Distributors in your MLM company who are not in your upline or downline.

Customer – A product buyer who is not authorized by the MLM company to sell products. They only purchase products and services for their personal use.

Diamond – A distributor who has reached an approximately 6 figure annual income from their chosen MLM business. The actual number can vary but they are usually considered higher leaders in the business. In this book, I use the term to represent such a level. Your MLM may have a different name depending on your rank structure.

Distributor – An independent person or company who sells network marketing products or the business opportunity to others.

Downline – Distributors that have enrolled as part of your network marketing team. You would earn a percentage of all their purchases and sales down to a company determined level based on your rank.

Dream building – A motivational activity where a person imagines their wildest dreams have materialized in real life.

Enroller – A distributor who has prospected and signed up the new distributor or customer. In some MLMs, enrollers and sponsors might earn different bonuses.

FDA – Abbreviation for Food and Drug Administration

Follow up calls – Contacting a prospect who has shown interest in building a business with or purchasing products.

GV – Group Volume (total points of your group) (See OV)

Leaders – Distributors who have sponsored several other independent distributors who want to build a network marketing business.

Legs – The column structure of placing distributors and/or customers under each other. Some MLMs provide bonuses to distributors with their desired network structures. See your compensation plan for details.

Levels – These are horizontal rows of distributors contained in any chosen leg level. Some MLMs pay higher bonuses depending on the numbers (or point values) of distributors or customers at the same level. See your compensation plan for details.

Limiting beliefs – Personal, often erroneous thoughts that inhibit personal and financial growth.

Mentor – A person who gently encourages and guides another person to become better in some way. The mentorship is usually more heart-centered in nature than a coach who focuses more on accountability.

MLM – Abbreviation for Multi-Level Marketing. I also use this term interchangeably with network marketing.

Home Classes – Classes where distributors educate and demonstrate the use of company products and/or services for the purse of enrolling both customers and distributors.

Product buyer – A person who just wants to buy products, they do not want to build a multi-level marketing business.

OV – Abbreviation for Overall Volume or Organizational Volume in some MLMs. (See GV)

Passive income – Money earned with minimal activity. Income earned independent of time, unlike a job where you are paid based on hours worked.

Place holder – Some MLM companies allow temporary placement of customers somewhere in the downline structure to generate sales but will be replaced as soon as possible with a business builder.

Placement moves – Moving a distributor or customer to another part of the downline structure to maximize income. (Permitted by some MLM companies)

Prospecting – Purposely interacting with people in order to generate interested in products or the business opportunity of the chosen MLM company.

PV – Short for Personal Volume or Point Value. The amount of points credited to a distributor based on product sales. PV levels can provide opportunity for increased rank and/or bonuses

Pyramid (Ponzi) scheme – An illegal business model that recruits individuals via promises of money or services. Sometimes called a Ponzi scheme where part of the "signup payment" goes directly to the enroller. Eventually, most Ponzi schemes collapse because people at the bottom never make money. Legal "pyramids" always base income from product flow, rather than just promises of income based on their investment at signup. If it seems too good, stay away!

QR code – Two-dimensional bar code read by smartphones and mobile devices to connects to a website or email address.

Rank – Levels of achievement based on your PV and team network structure. Usually, the higher the rank, the higher to bonuses paid. Note rank usually restarts at the lowest value each month and builds to the end of the month.

Results – A goal you commit to reach in either sponsoring and/or sales. When done weekly, tracking is more effective.

Retail – Products sold to customers at a percentage markup in price from the wholesale price. (See secret #10)

Retention rates – The rate at which you keep your customers. Usually measured in a rolling 90-day average. This is a good indicator of how easy or hard it will be to develop a sustainable MLM business. (e.g. 33% retention means a third of your customers keep ordering after 90 days.)

S.M.A.R.T. Goals – An acronym to help set and achieve goals: Specific, Measurable, Achievable, Relevant, Time-Bound. (See secret #5 – SMART WHY)

Show and tell - An activity to introduce products to prospects.

Starter Kit – A collection of products specially priced for new distributors or customers.

Simple Connector – The name of a simple CRM app designed to help MLM distributors collect, store, and follow up with prospects and team members.

Sponsor – A distributor with distributors and customers directly in their front-line and who earns bonuses from their purchases. In some MLMs they are distinct from Enrollers who are the distributor who prospected and signed them up.

Support activities – Work that is necessary for the smooth running of the business but does not involve other people and therefore does not directly generate income.

Team – All of your distributors and customers who, with your encouragement and help plus their effort and commitment, build businesses together. Also includes upline who help you with your team.

Upline – Distributors from your sponsor all the way up to the master distributor at the top of the entire network of an MLM company. They benefit financially, up to a pre-determined level set by their rank from your sales and efforts and therefore are ethically obligated to support you.

WHY – The personal driving force that motivates a person towards a goal. Your WHY is your fuel to build your dreams.

WOW – A demonstration to introduce your product or service to a prospect that causes them to say, "WOW, what was that? Please tell me more!" (See secret #5)

Zoom – A widely-used online video conferencing tool that is used to communicate both prospects, team members, and customers. Both free and paid accounts are available depending on needs. See: www.zoom.us

Index

About Ron Wilder

Ron Wilder is a network marketing advocate, published author, architect of various online MLM training programs, and mastermind behind the *Simple Connector™* CRM mobile app.

Ron's books help to make people's lives better by distilling the essence of complex topics in easy-to-understand ways. He especially enjoys helping network marketers find their WHYs to provide the fuel that helps them push past their fears to achieve the greatness they deserve.

As a retired Professional Engineer (PE) (thanks to network marketing), Ron also believes that technology and automation should simplify rather than complicate people's lives. He is the quintessential inventor and entrepreneur who enjoys creating powerful products that are simple, intuitive, and friendly for users.

Thank you very much for reading

Beyond the Products

Don't forget you can access all of the bonus gifts at:
www.BeyondTheProducts.com/bonuses

If you have any questions or comments
Please visit:
www.SimpleConnector.com/contact

For your free trial of our mobile MLM App,
Simple Connector™ CRM please visit
www.SimpleConnector.com/btp-gift

Made in the USA
Middletown, DE
29 October 2020